AMERICA
IN THE
KOREAN
WAR

EDWARD F. DOLAN

AMERICA
IN THE
KOREAN
WAR

The Millbrook Press

Brookfield, Connecticut

Cover photograph courtesy of National Archives

Photographs courtesy of Harry S. Truman Library: p. 17; UPI/Corbis-Bettmann: pp. 20, 32, 46, 53, 65, 78, 84, 91, 94 (both), 95 (bottom), 96 (top), 97, 102; Archive Photos: pp. 31, 57; National Archives: p. 44; Corbis-Bettmann: p. 95 (top); Corbis: p. 96 (bottom). Maps by Joe Le Monnier.

Library of Congress Cataloging-in-Publication Data
Dolan, Edward F., 1924–
America in the Korean War/Edward F. Dolan.
p.   cm.
Includes bibliographical references and index.
ISBN 0–7613–0361–8 (lib. bdg.)
1. Korean War, 1950–1953—Participation, American.
2. Korean War, 1950–1953—Armistices.
3. United States—Foreign relations—1945–1953.   I. Title
DS919.D65   1998
951.904'2—dc21   97–50460   CIP

Published by The Millbrook Press, Inc.
2 Old New Milford Road
Brookfield, Connecticut 06804

CONTENTS

AMERICA
IN THE
KOREAN
WAR

CHAPTER 1
JUNE 25, 1950

AT FOUR O'CLOCK IN THE MORNING of a rainy June 25, 1950, the South Korean soldiers heard a distant roar. For a moment, they thought it was the sound of a sudden thunderstorm. Then they were recoiling in shock and astonishment as artillery shells came crashing in on them, ripping up great chunks of earth.

The soldiers were stationed at points along the 38th Parallel, an invisible line that circles the globe at 38 degrees north latitude. It divided the former small nation of Korea into two smaller countries. The Communist-dominated and Soviet-backed Democratic People's Republic of Korea lay on its north side. Spreading away on the south was the Republic of Korea, a member of the United Nations. The two were known worldwide simply as North and South Korea.

With one a Communist state and the other a democracy, they were avowed enemies. Life for their troops on guard along each side of the Parallel had always been tense. At times, there had been skirmishes and artillery exchanges, especially when the northerners had crossed into the south to raid the rice paddies there for food. But, this morning, the South Korean troops (called ROKs, for the Republic of

Korea) knew that the shells pouring in on them had to mean something different. Something far more serious and deadly than another "rice raid."

They were right. At 5:00 A.M., long columns of North Korean tanks—Russian-built T34s sheathed in heavy armor plate and mounted with high velocity 85-millimeter (mm) cannons and machine guns—clanked into view on the muddy roads leading to the Parallel. Behind them came a flood of infantry troops. The South Koreans suddenly realized the truth. Their country was being invaded.

INVASION

Surging down to the Parallel was a force of 89,000 men under the command of General Chai Ung Jun—a force made up of seven infantry divisions, three independent infantry regiments, and 150 tanks. The attack struck at four points along the Parallel.

At its western end, several infantry units attacked and captured a small post on the isolated Ongjin peninsula. Some miles to the east, four divisions crossed into South Korea at a point about 30 miles (48 kilometers) above Seoul, its capital city. Two divisions struck midway along the Parallel, with one heading for the city of Chunchon, and the other moving toward Hongchon 20 miles (48 kilometers) farther on. Finally, at the eastern end of the line, a division speared southward along a coastal road.

Facing the onslaught were four ROK divisions. Totaling 38,000 men, they were far outnumbered by the enemy. To begin, they were all undermanned, a problem they shared with the rest of the ROK army because their country could not afford the cost of bringing its troops up to full strength. Making matters worse, the attack had come as a complete surprise. Everything had been peaceful along the Parallel for weeks. No one had been aware that the North Koreans were assembling a massive invasion force in the hills on its far side. Consequently, many of the ROK troops were away on

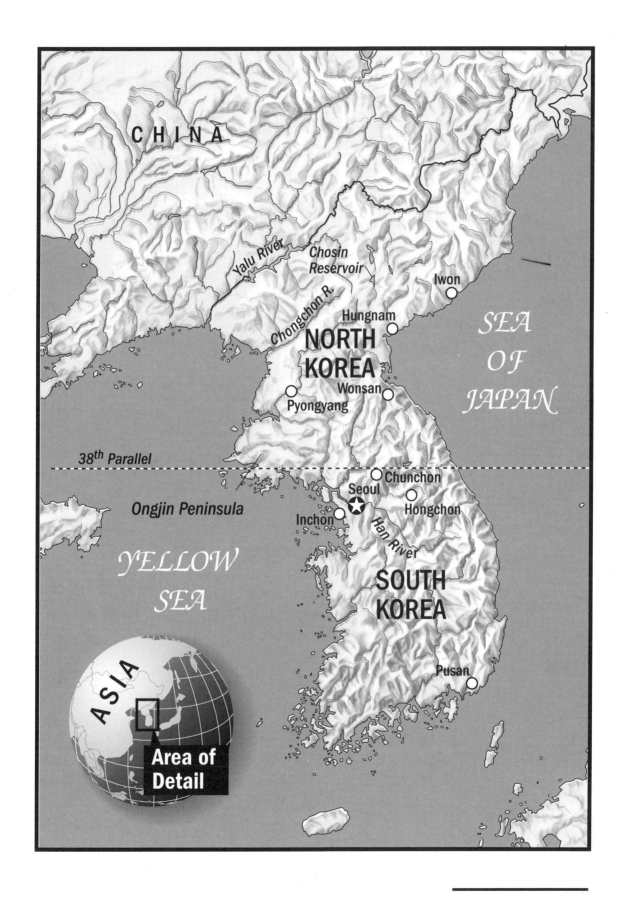

CHINA

Yalu River

Chosin
Reservoir

Chongchon R.

Iwon

Hungnam

NORTH
KOREA

Wonsan

Pyongyang

SEA
OF
JAPAN

38th Parallel

Ongjin Peninsula

Chunchon

Seoul

Hongchon

Inchon

Han River

*YELLOW
SEA*

SOUTH
KOREA

ASIA

Pusan

**Area of
Detail**

THE KOREAN PENINSULA

North and South Korea occupy the small Korean Peninsula. Bordered by China on the north and Russia on the far northeast, the peninsula stretches southward for 600 miles (966 kilometers) and measures about 200 miles (322 kilometers) across at its widest point and some 125 miles (201 kilometers) at its narrowest. On its west side lies the Yellow Sea. To the east, the Sea of Japan extends over to the Japanese home islands.

From the farms of each come rice, corn, barley, vegetables, and dairy products. North Korea's principal natural resources are coal, iron, and hydroelectric power. Coal and hydroelectric power are also among South Korea's natural resources, along with lead, tungsten, and graphite.

Prior to the division at the 38th Parallel, the peninsula was home to the single nation of Korea. The name Korea is derived from Koryo, a ruling dynasty that held power from 935 A.D. to 1392. Korea is also known to its people as Choson (sometimes also spelled Chosen), which means "Morning Calm."

The nation's history is thought to date from about 3000 B.C. It was ruled by various dynasties until being made a dependent state of China in the seventeenth century. The Chinese reign lasted until the late 1800s, when Japan became the predominant foreign power in Korea. Japan annexed the peninsula in 1910 and then had to give it up after being defeated in World War II. The division of the peninsula into North and South Korea soon followed.

weekend leave. Far fewer than 38,000 men were actually on duty to meet the onslaught.

Even worse, the four divisions were poorly equipped, again a problem shared by the entire ROK army. With just a few aging artillery pieces at hand, they were being hit by an enemy with three times as many guns. But, worst of all, the

ROKs could mount no defense against the invaders' most lethal weapons—the 150 T34 tanks. The South Koreans were without tanks of their own. Nor did they have any armor-piercing artillery shells, antitank land mines, or combat aircraft. All they could defend themselves with were some 57mm antitank guns and a few 2.36-inch rocket launchers (better known as bazookas). Both had been used by the Allied forces in World War II and were helpless against the thick-skinned T34s. The 57mm shells did not have the muscle to pierce the armor plating of the T34s. They could do harm only if they managed to hit a weak spot near the engine at the rear. The bazooka rockets simply exploded harmlessly against the armor plating or bounced away.

THE MAIN ATTACK

Making up the main force in the invasion were the troops that General Chai Ung Jun sent across the Parallel near Seoul. Their mission was to hasten the fall of South Korea by taking its capital city and sending its government leaders fleeing in search of safety. To attain his goal, Chai not only committed four of his seven divisions to the attack but also 120 of his 150 tanks.

As they plunged toward Seoul, his troops met a fierce but useless resistance. The T34s battered down log roadblocks and rolled over gun emplacements. Firing at the oncoming enemy, the ROK soldiers watched as their 57mm shells and bazooka rockets failed to slow the tanks. Some soldiers snatched up explosive charges, dashed forward, and hurled them at the clanking monsters. Others climbed up on the tanks and tried to drop hand grenades through their turrets.

Though a few T34s were damaged, all these efforts ended in disaster for the ROKs. The soldiers were either cut down by machine-gun fire from the tanks or picked off by the NK (North Korean) infantry advancing from the rear. The same tragedy befell the South Koreans wherever the tanks and infantry rolled over the troop positions and gun emplacements in their path. Soon, panic overtook many of the South Koreans, and they fled at the very sight of the invaders.

Only in one place along the Parallel did the South Koreans hold back the enemy that Sunday. The NK troops striking at Chunchon were without armored help because General Chai had assigned his remaining thirty tanks to the attack on nearby Hongchon. A South Korean division, firing from concrete pillboxes north of Chunchon, stalled the attackers for hours until Chai turned several T34s away from Hangchon and sent them to crush the Chunchon positions.

By 9:30 in the morning of the 25th, all of the enemy's leading troops were across the Parallel, with thousands more to follow throughout the day and night. In Seoul, the ROK command staff was frantically calling in troops from everywhere in the country to meet the invasion. Many were summoned to Seoul where, the next morning, the South Koreans hit the invaders with a counterattack in the hope of saving the capital.

The action went well at first, but only at first. The invaders were thrown back, but quickly took the upper hand again by sending their seemingly indestructible T34s crashing through the South Korean line. Seoul would fall two days later.

━━━━

The invasion came on a Sunday morning, but the day was Saturday, June 24, in the United States, because Korea lay on the far side of the international dateline. The grim news of what was happening reached the Department of State in Washington, D.C., at 9:30 that Saturday night, coming in a telegram from the U.S. Embassy at Seoul.

A half hour later, the telephone rang in President Harry S. Truman's home at Independence, Missouri, where he was vacationing. The President picked up the receiver and heard the voice of Secretary of State Dean Acheson.

The United States, with World War II barely five years in the past, was about to be plunged into a new conflict.

CHAPTER 2
INTO THE WAR

PRESIDENT TRUMAN FLEW BACK TO WASHINGTON the next day. While he was en route, the United States asked the Security Council of the United Nations to meet in an emergency session to discuss the Korean crisis. The Council members confirmed the details of the invasion and branded it a breach of world peace. They then enacted a resolution calling for the North Korean government to cease hostilities and withdraw its troops back across the 38th Parallel.

An unusual circumstance enabled the group to develop the resolution without a problem. According to the rules of the United Nations, any measure that came to a vote before the Council members (eleven at the time) could be defeated by the veto of just one of their number. The Soviet Union (USSR) was a member and would have surely rejected a proposal aimed against a fellow Communist state. But the Soviet delegate, Jacob Malik, was not present at that night's session. He was boycotting the UN because it had recently turned down his request to have Communist China admitted to the organization. And so the resolution passed easily.

The Council members, however, were certain that the resolution would bear no fruit. North Korea would surely ignore it. They were right. The NK troops pressed into Seoul and took the city, routing its defenders and causing the South Korean government to flee southward.

TRUMAN TAKES ACTION

Immediately on arriving in Washington, President Truman held the first of two meetings with Secretary of State Acheson and other advisers to decide what the United States should do about the crisis far across the Pacific. Present were the secretary of defense, the secretaries of the Army, Navy, and Air Force, and the members of the military's Joint Chiefs of Staff, led by their chairman, General Omar N. Bradley.

All the men present shared three views. First, they recognized the invasion as an obvious move to broaden communism's hold on Asia by crushing South Korea's democratic government. Next, they felt that any U.S. effort to stem the invasion could see the nation plunged into a war with the Soviet Union and China, the region's two great Communist powers who would surely come to North Korea's aid. Finally, they shared the President's belief that the Soviet Union was behind the attack. (The puzzle of whether the Soviet Union ordered the invasion has never been answered. What has become known is that the Soviets' supreme leader, Josef Stalin, knew of the planned invasion and gave it his approval.)

Since 1945, the USSR had strengthened communism's grip on Europe by winning control of Poland, Hungary, Romania, and Czechoslovakia, customarily doing so by promoting Communist takeovers within their borders. Now it was using North Korea to smash the ROK government, certain that the United States would be so reluctant to ignite a third world war that it would not go to the little state's defense. America, Truman said, could not let that happen. The nation had to help South Korea.

President Truman, on the left, and Secretary of State Dean Acheson.

The invasion had caught the United States completely by surprise. To all who worked with him, the President was known as a man willing to make decisions—and make them quickly. He lived up to his reputation during that first meeting and the one that followed it the next day. He met the invasion with several steps that were recommended by Acheson and supported by all the other advisers.

He began with an order to General Douglas MacArthur, the commander of the occupation forces in Japan. The general was to send Air Force and Navy planes out to protect the American civilians being evacuated from Seoul by the U.S. Embassy. More than 1,500 Americans and some 500 other foreign nationals were hurried off to Japan by ship and aircraft.

Truman then called for military supplies to be sent to South Korea from U.S. depots in Japan. He also authorized American planes to support the ROK troops and protect the movement of the supplies from Japan. He stipulated, however, that all air actions be carried out south of the 38th Parallel. No planes were to venture into the north.

Next, the President had Acheson go to the Security Council and ask for the passage of a new and stronger resolution. As Seoul was falling far across the world, the Council acceded to the request. Adopted, with the Soviets' Jacob Malik again absent, was a resolution urging that "the members of the United Nations furnish such assistance" to South Korea "as may be necessary to repel the armed attacks and to restore international peace and security to the area."

The resolution pleased Truman. He had asked Acheson to seek it for the same reason that he had ordered all U.S. planes to remain below the 38th Parallel. He did not want to strike at North Korea on his own and enable the world's neutral countries to brand America as a giant bully attacking a tiny state. Instead, he wanted any move against North Korea to be carried out by the United Nations, making it a global effort to end an aggression. The resolution gave him what he wanted.

Though worried that he was risking a major war, the President knew that he was doing what had to be done to protect a threatened state. And he knew, from press reports and remarks made to him by congressional leaders, that he had the support of Congress and a great segment of the American public, both of whom were alarmed by the spread of communism worldwide. Above all else, he knew that he was doing a complete about-face in the nation's recent policies toward South Korea.

To see that about-face, we have to go back to the close of World War II.

AMERICA AND SOUTH KOREA

In 1945, four decades of Japanese rule in Korea came to an end. Japan had gained control of the small country in 1904, but had been forced to hand it over to American and Soviet occupation forces after being defeated in World War II.

With the 38th Parallel temporarily dividing Korea into two occupation zones, the Americans entered the southern region while the Soviets took over in the north. Both were to disarm the Japanese troops in their respective areas and supervise Korea's affairs until the country could be reunited as a free and independent country. (In two wartime conferences—in 1943 and 1945—the major nations fighting Germany and Japan had agreed to the Korean reunification.)

Early efforts to reunite Korea, however, failed when the Soviets sealed off their zone from the south. In 1947, at America's request, the United Nations developed a reunification plan. It called for an election to be held throughout Korea, with the people voting to select the members of a national assembly that would draft a democratic constitution and then establish a national government in keeping with the constitution. The election was to be held under the supervision of a special UN commission.

But the plan fell apart when the Soviets refused to allow the commission members to enter the northern zone. The American authorities went ahead with the UN election in May 1948. The result: the establishment in August of the Republic of Korea, with Syngman Rhee as its president. As soon as the new government took shape, the U.S. withdrew its occupation force of 50,000, leaving behind a handful of soldiers to serve as advisers to the ROK army.

In September 1948, the Soviet command and the north's Communist party established the Democratic People's Republic of Korea, with its capital the city of Pyongyang. The action was taken without UN participation. Kim Il Sung, the head of the Communist party, was named premier. The USSR began to remove its occupation forces.

General Douglas MacArthur and President Syngman Rhee of Korea at the August 15, 1948, ceremony declaring Korea a republic.

Two new states now glared at each other across the 38th Parallel. Only the south's Republic of Korea was recognized by the United Nations as the legal government of Korea.

By 1948, the world was caught up in what the press quickly called the "Cold War." It was a political and ideological struggle that pitted the United States and the world's free countries against the Soviet Union and its fellow Communist states. The struggle was to rage for four decades before ending with the collapse of communism in the early 1990s.

In March 1947, Congress heard President Truman deliver one of the most significant speeches of his career. In it, he outlined the strategy that America would employ in fighting the Cold War. It had been devised by General George C.

TRUMAN, TAIWAN, AND CHINA

In addition to the steps being taken against North Korea, President Truman called for an action directed at the Communist government on mainland China and the Chinese Nationalist government on the island of Taiwan (widely known at that time as Formosa). He ordered the U.S. Navy's 7th Fleet to enter the waters between the mainland and Taiwan to discourage the two foes from attacking each other.

Truman's action stemmed from the fact that, in 1949, after years of civil war, the Chinese Communists finally drove Generalissimo Chiang Kai-shek and his Nationalist government from the mainland. He had fled 115 miles (185 kilometers) across Taiwan Strait (also known as Formosa Strait) to Taiwan and had installed his government there. In 1950, it was widely thought that the Communist Chinese were preparing to attack Taiwan, put an end to Chiang's government, and reunite the island with the mainland. At the same time, Chiang Kai-shek, loudly proclaiming that he represented China's only legal government, was threatening to strike the mainland and unseat the Communists.

Though Truman's action was aimed at both the mainland and Taiwan governments, it was meant in greater part to discourage an attack on Taiwan. The President and his advisers suspected that the South Korean invasion might be the opening salvo in a general Communist campaign in Asia—and perhaps Europe—with the takeover of Taiwan as one of its aims. Their suspicion eventually proved to be groundless.

Marshall, then the secretary of state, along with Acheson (Marshall's undersecretary at the time) and other members of the State Department. It quickly became known as the Truman Doctrine.

The President described it as a strategy of "containment," meaning that the United States was dedicated to halting—"containing"—the spread of communism everywhere in the world. Whenever a country was faced with the threat of a Communist subversion or military action, America would provide economic and military aid to make the country strong enough to overcome the danger.

Operating under the Truman Doctrine, the country first granted $400 million to Greece and Turkey in 1947; the funds enabled both countries to resist impending takeovers. Next, Washington launched another of General Marshall's ideas—an economic plan, named in his honor, that provided Europe's wartorn nations with $12 billion to rebuild themselves so that they could gain the strength needed to resist the Communist encroachments in their midst. Then, in 1949, the United States participated in the formation of the North Atlantic Treaty Organization (NATO), which bound together twelve nations (later expanded to sixteen) in a pact to oppose any future aggressions in Europe by the Soviet Union.

Between 1948 and 1950, however, one country did not benefit from the Truman Doctrine: the infant Republic of South Korea. In those years, U.S. aid was sent to the republic, but not the type that it needed and wanted—offensive military gear. Modern tanks, artillery, and aircraft were not offered. All that arrived were small shipments of aging defensive weaponry. With so little equipment arriving, the ROK army was left weak and ill-armed.

There were two main reasons for the meager shipments. First, the United States felt that it had to place the bulk of its military equipment where it was most needed—in Europe, where the Soviet Union was making so many advances. Located far from this danger point (even though most of Asia was heavily communistic), the Republic of Korea struck many American leaders as a backwater that did not pose the threat of a Communist explosion.

The second reason had to do with the republic's seventy-five-year-old president, Syngman Rhee. A patriot who had resisted the Japanese and then the Communists for decades, Rhee was dedicated to seeing Korea reborn as a single nation. But he was a belligerent personality who alarmed the United States with his boast that, given the proper equipment (planes, tanks, and gasoline) he would invade North Korea and be rid of its Communist government in two weeks. Fearful that he would trigger a third world war, America made sure that he did not get the arms he so desperately wanted.

THE FINAL STEPS TO WAR

But now, with the attack on South Korea, the American attitude was suddenly transformed. In addition to the steps he was taking, President Truman asked General MacArthur to watch the fighting closely and report on how the South Koreans were faring.

Though Seoul had fallen and the South Korean army was in flight, Truman had not yet committed U.S. ground forces to the fighting. He hoped that, by providing military supplies and air support, he could somehow handle the Korean problem and avoid igniting a full-scale war. As he put it, the United States was not undertaking a war but a "police action," a limited effort meant to get the North Koreans back into their own country.

It was MacArthur who caused him to change his mind about the use of ground troops. While Seoul was falling, the general flew from his headquarters in Tokyo to Korea for a firsthand look at the battlefront. Landing near the capital and then driving to its outskirts, he was shocked by the devastation that the North Koreans were wreaking. He reported that they were plunging across Seoul's Han River. Amidst fleeing refugees and retreating soldiers, some ROK units were fiercely trying to fend off the attackers. But they were hopelessly outnumbered and without the help of thousands of their comrades who were in terrified flight with the refugees. They would never keep the enemy from overrunning them and spearing clear down to Korea's southern coast. U.S. troops would have to come to their aid if the entire country was not to be lost.

MacArthur's report caused the President to wire him a new set of orders on June 30: MacArthur was to begin rushing men to the battlefront. Truman also freed all U.S. aircraft for attacks on military installations north of the 38th Parallel. And he told the Navy to throw up a blockade along the Korean coasts and to bombard enemy positions ashore.

___

The die was now cast. The United States was going to war. Coming behind were the first of fifteen UN countries that had responded to the Security Council's resolution of June 27 by pledging to join the fighting.

Truman himself would never refer to it as a war, but always called it "the Korean conflict," because he did not request a formal declaration of war from Congress. If South Korea was to be saved, he had no time to wait for the debate that would necessarily precede a congressional declaration. As a result, Congress never formally declared war on North Korea, but it was nevertheless to be a war, and indeed a vicious one.

CHAPTER 3
FIRST BLOOD

A T THE TIME HE WAS TOLD to commit ground troops to the fighting, General MacArthur had the Eighth Army on occupation duty in Japan. It consisted mainly of four infantry divisions. The 24th Division became the first of their number to send men to Korea when he ordered one of its battalions to speed to the battlefront.

TASK FORCE SMITH

The 406 men in the unit, which was soon to be nicknamed Task Force Smith for its commander, Lieutenant Colonel Charles Smith, flew to the city of Pusan on Korea's southeastern tip, landing on July 1 and immediately moving north. Under orders to travel as far as possible from Pusan before digging in to meet the oncoming enemy, they were on a deadly but all-important mission. They were to be the first Americans to do battle with the invaders. As such, they were vital to a strategy that MacArthur was already developing for winning the war.

What was that strategy? Pusan boasted South Korea's finest port. MacArthur knew that it was the invaders' chief target. Should they capture the city, South Korea would be totally in their hands and all of Korea would be reunited—as a Communist state. But, if he could save the port, he would be in the position to stage a daring counterattack that he had devised. It would devastate the North Koreans and hurl them back across the 38th Parallel.

But he needed time to prepare for the attack, and time to bring enough men and arms in from Japan to save Pusan. The soldiers of Task Force Smith were to start buying that time for him. They were to spread themselves across the invaders' path and slow the southward thrust until more men were brought in to defend the city.

Colonel Smith and his men arrived at a point 3 miles (5 kilometers) above the town of Osan on the night of July 4. Here, about 50 miles (80 kilometers) south of Seoul, they found the perfect terrain for a defensive action: two hills standing to either side of the main road running down from the broken capital. Smith's force was now up to 540 men. Joining him were 134 soldiers and six howitzers from a field artillery battalion. The newcomers had sailed from Japan aboard landing craft and had then raced to his side.

Smith knew that while he had been on the move, the NKs had crossed the Han River and were now marching directly toward him. He spent the night placing his troops on the high ground to either side of the roadway. Into position went the infantrymen with their rifles and machine guns. The unit's single antitank gun took its place between and behind them. A mile farther back, the six howitzers were rolled into a line. Then the men settled down to await the enemy.

During the wait, Smith wondered how his troops would perform when the enemy finally arrived. His tiny force would be hopelessly outnumbered and outgunned. Worse, with the exception of a few of his officers who had fought in World War II, it was made up of young recruits who had never been in battle. Further, like all the occupation troops in Japan, they had received hardly any combat training because trouble of any kind had never been anticipated. And, for the same reason, they were not armed with the latest in weapons. In all, they were ill-equipped and ill-trained soldiers who had been suddenly yanked out of comfortable quarters in Japan and thrust into the face of death. How would they now act?

OSAN: THE FIRST BATTLE

On the rainy morning of July 5, a column of thirty-three T34 tanks lumbered into view in the far distance. Leading them were eight tanks, all moving abreast; those behind were ranged across the road in lines of four each.

Smith's howitzers opened the first U.S. battle of the war when the tanks were 2,000 yards (1,828 meters) away. Shells screamed overhead and began to rain down on the T34s, ripping up great clouds of mud near some and making direct hits on others. The infantrymen cheered and then groaned on seeing the direct hits. The shells, like those of the ROKs at the start of the invasion, did not have the power to stop the tanks. The T34s kept moving.

Ignoring everything that the Americans threw at them, they lumbered past Smith's infantrymen in two waves. Two of the leaders in the first wave finally rolled up into the face of his antitank gun. Six shells erupted from the gun. All scored direct hits. The T34s bucked to a stop. One exploded in flames. Its turret flew open. Out came two North Koreans with their arms held high in surrender.

Then a third North Korean burst through the turret, firing a burp gun as he emerged. The bullets smashed into a nearby machine-gun nest. One American (his name remains unknown to this day) pitched over and became the first U.S. soldier to die in the Korean fighting. A moment later, the North Korean lay dead, killed by the survivors manning the machine gun.

Now the rest of the tanks came smashing past the antitank gun, continuously firing their cannons and machine guns as they swept by. Then they were behind Smith, cutting him off from an easy means of escape.

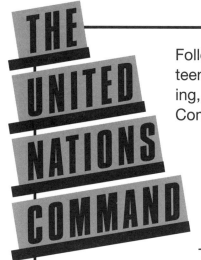

THE UNITED NATIONS COMMAND

Following the Security Council's resolution of July 7, fifteen nations committed themselves to the Korean fighting, with some immediately joining the United Nations Command and others coming later. The fifteen were:

Australia	France	New Zealand
Belgium	Great Britain	The Philippines
Canada	Greece	Thailand
Colombia	Luxembourg	Turkey
Ethiopia	The Netherlands	South Africa

Their contributions to the fighting were widely varied. Together, Australia, Canada, Great Britain, and New Zealand sent 40,000, with Great Britain also placing the warships of its Far Eastern Station under MacArthur's command. The Philippines contributed 5,000 infantrymen. Belgium, Colombia, France, and Ethiopia each contributed a battalion. Greece also assigned a battalion, plus an air transport squadron. Tiny Luxembourg came up with an infantry regiment.

Five nations with strong neutrality policies did not send troops but contributed mercy missions. Denmark assigned a hospital ship to Korean waters. An ambulance came from India, and field hospitals from Sweden, Norway, and Italy.

The United States and South Korea made the greatest contributions. In mid-July, South Korean President Syngman Rhee handed the entire ROK army (at the time, down to some 42,000 men but due to grow to more than 400,000 by the dawn of 1953) to MacArthur. The United States committed the greatest number of all—more than 5.7 million men and women of the Army, Navy, Marine Corps, Coast Guard, and Air Force.

But the worst was yet to come. Soon after the tanks had passed, Smith sighted a column of infantry 6 miles (10 kilometers) long—10,000 men in all. It was then that he learned how his men would fight. Some, though terrified at their first taste of war, would perform valiantly. Others would turn and flee.

When the first North Koreans flooded into the pass between the two hills, Smith shouted the order to open fire. As new to battle as they were, most of his young soldiers reacted instantly, bringing their arms to bear in a concentrated fire that threw back the enemy.

It was but a momentary victory. There were simply too many NKs for Task Force Smith to handle. The attackers surged up the hill on the west side of the road and sent the defenders sprinting over to the opposite hill. No sooner had they made their way there than the enemy flowed around its base and began attacking from all sides.

The Americans stubbornly fought off the assault for three hours before Smith decided that further resistance would achieve nothing but the loss of his men. He ordered them to break off the action. They began to retreat toward Osan, only to run into the nightmare of having the enemy catch them in a deadly crossfire from the sides of the road. Firing back and protecting each other as best they could, the Americans finally escaped beyond the range of the enemy guns. The North Koreans did not pursue them.

And so the first American battle in the Korean War ended in tragic failure. Of the 540 men who faced the North Koreans that July day, Smith lost 150 while the artillery battalion suffered 31 lost—listed as killed, wounded, or missing. The battle had been a terrible but valiant one for the small task force. Many of Smith's young recruits had courageously held their ground for as long as possible in the face of overwhelming enemy numbers. Their stand was to go down as one of the finest U.S actions in the Korean fighting.

A NEW RESOLUTION

As Task Force Smith was retreating, the UN Security Council met to discuss and then enact a new Korean resolution (with the Soviets' Malik still absent).

It contained three parts. First, it authorized the formation of a United Nations Command to fight the war. Next, it addressed the member nations that wished to join the struggle; they were to make their forces available to the United States. Finally, it named President Truman as the executive agent of the UN in pursuing the war and asked him to appoint a commander for the United Nations Command. As expected, the post went to MacArthur.

The measure placed the United States, which would contribute the most men to the fighting, in charge of the war, with Truman, as executive agent, being responsible for conducting it. MacArthur, as head of the United Nations Command, would lead all U.S. Army, Navy, Air Force, and Marine personnel in Korea, the ROK forces, and the troops, ships, planes, and medical aid sent by the fifteen UN nations that joined the United Nations Command.

THE TERRIBLE DAYS

The battle at Osan marked the start of a terrible July for MacArthur's force. In Tokyo, the general watched his outnumbered Americans suffer one defeat after another.

Stubbornly, MacArthur continued preparing for his planned counterattack.

On sweeping through Osan, the North Koreans met newly arrived units of the 24th Division and drove them back from four towns: Pyongtaek, Ansong, Chonan, and Taejon. The raw Americans behaved as had the men of Task Force Smith. Some retreated. Some were so nervous that they could not respond quickly when ordered to open fire. But most fought back valiantly, doing their best to slow a giant army—and at times succeeding.

It was miraculous that they were able to slow the enemy at all. Not only were they facing overwhelming numbers but also the worst of battle conditions. The monsoon season was upon Korea, and the fighting was taking place in heavy rains followed by periods of intense heat that sent temperatures above 100° F (38°C). It was weather that caused weapons to rust, men to weaken from heat, and uniforms to rot.

By mid-July, the invaders were spread all across the width of South Korea. The troops that had struck midway along the 38th Parallel were now far south and had linked up with the invasion's main force. Units from the main force were fanning out and thrusting down South Korea's western side. The troops that crossed the Parallel on the east coast were fighting their way along the shoreline road.

Pusan seemed certain to fall.

U.S. Marines slog through one of the thousands of rice paddies that stretch across the South Korean landscape. The paddies were fertilized with human waste, and soldiers who were thirsty enough to ignore the stench were soon violently ill with dysentery.

AMERICA GOES TO WAR

The United States was ill-prepared for the Korean War. At the close of World War II, in 1945, Americans everywhere wanted nothing more than to return to peacetime life.

The government, responding to this desire, quickly released thousands of men from the armed forces so that they could get on with their schooling, their careers, and their family lives. Just as quickly, U.S. factories turned from the wartime production of tanks, planes, ships, and munitions to the peacetime manufacture of everything from automobiles to refrigerators. The nation entered a boom period in home construction as thousands of new neighborhoods took shape for young veterans and their families.

On July 18, 1950, these young men are sworn into the Marine Corps, knowing full well that they will be seeing action soon. By August, more than a quarter of a million men had either enlisted or been returned to service.

Consequently, when the war erupted in June 1950, the number of personnel in the armed forces was down to a bed-rock level and the military equipment in use was outdated, left over from World War II. For example, MacArthur's four occupation divisions in Japan were getting by with two rather than three battalions per regiment. Artillery battalions could boast just two rather than the customary three batteries.

But the nation quickly threw itself into the war. Men in reserve and National Guard units who had fought in World War II were summoned back into uniform. The selective-service system was extended, enabling the government to recruit young men for the fighting. The training of all troops intensifed, with the result that, just a few months later, they again ranked among the best-trained soldiers in the world.

They were also the best equipped in the world. Throughout the Korean fighting, U.S. manufacturers provided the military with a steady stream of modern equipment and arms while at the same time continuing to produce the civilian products that the nation's people desired. In all, the United States was to expend $15 billion on the war.

Most Americans at first supported the country's defense of South Korea. Ever since World War II, they had watched communism's global advances and had felt that America, despite the Truman Doctrine, had not done enough to stop them. Many also believed the widespread rumors (eventually proved groundless) that the federal government was riddled with Communists or Communist sympathizers who hoped for the eventual overthrow of the nation.

Truman's actions on behalf of South Korea sent a wave of hope through the nation. At last, the United States was taking a firm stand against a Communist aggression. This initial feeling about their country's participation in the fighting, however, was to change to hatred for the war during the next three years.

But that was not to happen. Although the Americans were still taking a beating, the tide of battle was turning in their favor. MacArthur, knowing that Pusan had to be saved if his counterattack was to work, committed more and more troops to the field. Units from the 25th and 7th Divisions in Japan arrived at the front. The lst Cavalry Division (now an infantry outfit though it retained its name from the days when it had been a horse-mounted unit) also crossed over from Japan, plus a Marine brigade that would soon be designated as the 5th Marines. President Syngman Rhee, who had moved south when Seoul fell, was reassembling his scattered ROK units and placing them in MacArthur's hands. Finally, the UN countries that had pledged to join the fighting were sending their first troops, planes, and warships to Korea. MacArthur's army was fast becoming a true United Nations Command.

The Command's growing strength was also being felt in other ways. Equipment was pouring in from Japan and the United States. American, British, and Australian planes were daily strafing and bombing North Korean positions and supply convoys. The NK troops advancing down the east coast were being battered by shellfire from the warships that had gathered offshore.

All these actions could not help but weaken the North Koreans. But there were additional reasons for their waning strength. They were suffering losses that would soon total 60,000 and were as exhausted as their foe by the fighting, the rainstorms, and the intolerable heat. And they were far hungrier than the enemy. Their supply line, running clear back to North Korea, was stretched ominously thin and under constant air attack. Food and munitions were agonizingly slow in reaching the front lines.

Though weakening, the NK troops continued to press toward Pusan, coming up against Lieutenant General Walton H. Walker. He had long commanded the Eighth Army on occupation duty in Japan and was now in charge of the Korean ground action. His troops were banded together under the Eighth Army banner and were steadily increasing in number. Before long, he would have under his command the four U.S. occupation divisions, the Marine brigade, the UN contingents, and five ROK divisions.

Because of the Eighth Army's steady growth, Walker was able to establish a lengthy defensive line in front of Pusan. Called the Pusan Perimeter, it started on the east coast about 80 miles (129 kilometers) north of the city, ran westward for some 60 miles (96 kilometers), and turned left to spear down to Korea's southern coast. Once the line was in place, Walker's troops spent the rest of July successfully holding it against a series of NK attacks. At times, the North Koreans burst through, but were always flung back by a force that was at last outnumbering them. By early August, there were 92,000 troops (including ROK and British) inside the Perimeter. Outside were 70,000 North Koreans.

Despite the imbalance in strength, the North Koreans launched an all-out offensive against Pusan in late August. They knifed through at several points and took the towns of Taegu, just 50 miles (80 kilometers) from Pusan, and nearby Miryang, only to have the Eighth Army troops push them back to the Perimeter line. With these NK defeats, Pusan was at last made safe from capture.

The weakening North Koreans continued to pound uselessly at the Perimeter during early September. MacArthur watched the fighting with grim satisfaction. The two conditions that were needed to make his counteroffensive work were at last in place. The North Koreans had stretched their supply lines too thin, and they had failed to take Pusan. It was time to attack.

He struck on September 15 far behind the enemy lines.

CHAPTER 4

INCHON

AS SOON AS AMERICA ENTERED THE WAR, MacArthur selected the target he would hit when the time came for his counterattack. Once the North Koreans had advanced far south from Seoul, he would stage an invasion miles to their rear. He would sail in from the Yellow Sea and take the port city of Inchon, just 20 miles (32 kilometers) west of Seoul.

From there, he would plunge inland, recapture Seoul, and sever the NK supply lines. Then, when the enemy troops on the Pusan Perimeter had to turn and dash back to fight him off, he would have the Eighth Army come chasing after them. Caught between two massive forces, they would be doomed.

It has always been wise strategy to attack behind the enemy, but MacArthur's idea appalled the Joint Chiefs of Staff when they heard of it. They had a single shocked reaction: He could not have picked a worse spot than the harbor at Inchon for an amphibious invasion.

Why?

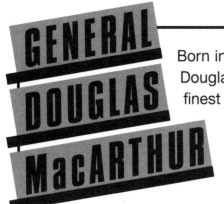

GENERAL DOUGLAS MacARTHUR

Born in 1880, the son of a distinguished army officer, Douglas MacArthur etched for himself one of the finest careers in U.S. military history. He graduated first in his class from West Point in 1903 and rose steadily through the ranks until he was named a brigadier general during the fighting in World War I. He became full general in 1930, and was named military adviser to the Philippines in 1935.

MacArthur retired in 1937 but remained in the Philippines, building the strength of that country's small army. He had been given its command earlier by Philippine President Manuel Queson.

President Franklin D. Roosevelt recalled the general for service in 1941 as war was threatening in the Pacific. When the fighting erupted, MacArthur first defended the Philippines but was ordered to Australia by Roosevelt to become the supreme commander in the Southwest Pacific Theater. He led the drive back to the Philippines, which had fallen to the Japanese, was named supreme commander of all U.S. Army forces in the Pacific, and prepared to attack Japan.

The war ended abruptly with the dropping of the atomic bomb on Japan, and MacArthur accepted the Japanese surrender aboard the battleship U.S.S. *Missouri* in Tokyo Bay on September 5, 1945. He then served as commander of the occupation forces in Japan and introduced measures that changed the course of that nation's history—among them land reforms, recognition of women's rights, the country's disarmament, and a new and democratic constitution.

MacArthur was a flamboyant man of dramatic ways. His regal behavior, along with his military expertise, impressed many of his fellow officers. But his manner irritated, or amused, just as many others.

INCHON HARBOR

To begin, Inchon's harbor was located far from the sea. Before ever reaching the port, MacArthur's warships and transports would have to advance slowly along a 10-mile (16 kilometer) waterway called "Flying Fish Channel," with mud flats stretching away on either side. Then, at the end of the channel, the invaders would find the harbor entrance guarded by Wolmi-do Island ("Moon Tip Island"). A 300-foot (91-meter) hill rose from the island's center and bristled with artillery that—joined by guns on the hills of the city—could blast the invasion fleet to bits.

Further, Flying Fish Channel was narrow and its current swift; both features could make it almost impossible for his armada to reach the harbor without some kind of accident. Then there were Inchon's monster tides. During the times of the year when they were at their worst, they could raise the harbor's water level by more than 30 feet (9 meters). But when they rolled back out, they left the mud flats exposed. If caught in a low tide, his landing force would be stuck in the mud for hours until the next high tide, easy prey for the enemy gunners on shore.

MacArthur ignored these dangers and continued laying his invasion plans. He meant to attack on a rising tide and knew that he needed at least a 29-foot tide for his ships to remain afloat. There were three periods left in 1950 when the waters would be high enough for his purposes. The first one fell on September 15. He chose that day for the landing.

But he continued to hear a flood of objections from the Joint Chiefs and other high-ranking officers: Flying Fish Channel was probably mined; if just one of his ships was crippled there, it would create a traffic jam that could end the operation in an instant. If some problem delayed the landing, the tide would ebb, turning his ships and men into sitting targets. He should choose a more accessible spot.

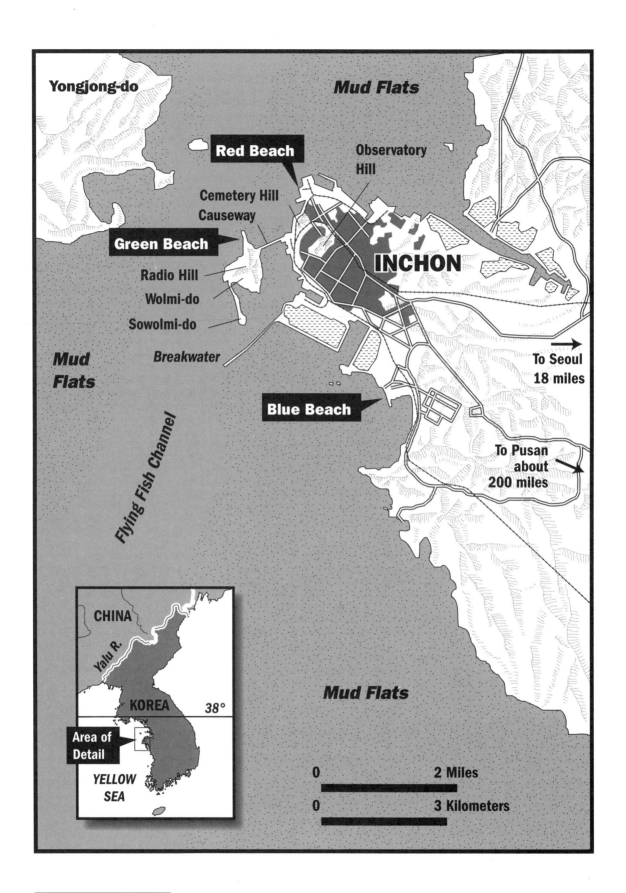

Yongjong-do

Mud Flats

Red Beach

Observatory Hill

Cemetery Hill Causeway

Green Beach

Radio Hill

Wolmi-do

Sowolmi-do

Breakwater

INCHON

To Seoul
18 miles

Blue Beach

To Pusan
about
200 miles

*Mud
Flats*

Flying Fish Channel

Mud Flats

CHINA

Yalu R.

KOREA

38°

Area of
Detail

*YELLOW
SEA*

0   2 Miles

0   3 Kilometers

MacArthur stubbornly countered all the arguments. Inchon would give him the best chance for success because he would catch the enemy commanders completely off guard; like his own people, they would think that no sane man would dare attack the city from the sea. Also the plan offered the best chance to retake Seoul quickly and sever the North Koreans' lifeline at the greatest distance from their front lines.

The Inchon landing, he predicted, would save the 100,000 lives that would be lost if he struck elsewhere or was forced to launch the counterattack from Pusan. It was certain to be a success. But if anything did go wrong, he would quickly order a withdrawal to save lives.

Voicing his views in his usual dramatic fashion and with one of the most remarkable careers in U.S. military history giving them added weight, the general finally won the day. On July 18, President Truman gave him permission to proceed with the Inchon landing.

TO INCHON

MacArthur assembled 70,000 troops and more than 250 ships and transports for the invasion. Assigned to the campaign were the U.S. 7th Division (on occupation duty in Japan), the 1st Marine Division (called in from the United States), the 5th Marines (the brigade that was presently fighting on the Pusan Perimeter), and a contingent of ROK Marines. The force was named X (10th) Corps and was placed under the command of Major General Edward Almond, who had been serving as MacArthur's chief of staff in Japan.

The invasion fleet was made up of 194 American warships and a collection of vessels from Britain, Canada, New Zealand, and France. In addition, there were several hundred small craft that would carry the troops to the shore.

The majority of Almond's men sailed for Inchon from Japan in early September. They were met near Pusan by the ships carrying the 5th Marines and, at other points, by warships approaching from various stations. MacArthur, sailing aboard a destroyer, joined the fleet in the Yellow Sea as it was nearing its destination.

Though he was supremely confident that success lay ahead for his X Corps, there was one aspect of the invasion that had long troubled the general—the artillery on Wolmi-do Island. Unless he managed to silence those guns, they would raise havoc with his fleet. But it was too big a job to leave until invasion day. Wolmi-do had to be defanged beforehand.

But how could he do that without tipping off the North Koreans that Inchon was the target of a major operation? He chose a simple strategy. In the weeks before mid-September, he staged a series of naval bombardments and air raids at points on South Korea's east and west coasts, with Inchon and Wolmi-do among them. The ruse worked. The North Koreans, not knowing where a possible attack might strike—or even *if* an attack was planned—did not send troops to protect Inchon.

TWO PRE-INVASION ATTACKS

At dawn on September 13, two days before the scheduled landing, a small armada of American and British ships continued the bombardment of Wolmi-do. Six destroyers broke away from the invasion fleet that was now gathering some miles offshore, sailed into Flying Fish Channel, and cautiously proceeded to Wolmi-do in single file. To the surprise of their crews, all was quiet on the island. Neither its guns nor those in the city greeted their approach. Either the North Koreans did not know, or did not believe, that Inchon was under a serious threat. The destroyers stopped several hundred yards off shore and brought their guns to bear on the target. Then they opened fire.

Instantly, trees were shredded on Wolmi-do. Debris shot into the air. Thick clouds of smoke rolled skyward. For three minutes, the stunned North Korean gunners did not answer the onslaught. Then flashes of light burst through the smoke. The island's biggest guns sent 75mm shells hurtling in on the destroyers. Two ships took a total of eight direct hits: one suffered so much damage that it had to drop out of the action.

The flashes on Wolmi-do betrayed the positions of its biggest guns and the destroyers wasted no time in silencing them. Then they shifted their fire to the smaller gun emplacements. Finally, leaving the island blackened and silent, the ships departed and made their way back to sea. They returned the next day, this time joined by a flight of warplanes. The planes dove in on Wolmi-do and blanketed it with a cascade of bombs. The destroyers pounded both the island and Inchon itself.

Then it was September 15.

THE LANDINGS

MacArthur's plans called for General Almond's X Corps to land at three points, which were designated as "Beaches"—Green, Red, and Blue. Green Beach was located on Wolmi-do and was to be hit by elements of the 5th Marines. Red Beach, a strip of waterfront on the mainland north of Wolmi-do, would also be hit by 5th Marine units, with the 7th Division to land later for the advance on Seoul. Blue Beach at the southern edge of Inchon was assigned to the 1st Marine Division.

The three landings were not to be made all at the same time. Rather, Wolmi-do would be hit first, on the morning's rising tide, with the assaults of Red and Blue Beaches coming hours later—at sunset—on the next high tide. Wolmi-do had to be taken first because, despite the poundings of the past days, it still posed a major threat. There could still be some active batteries remaining on the island. They had to be silenced and their danger to the troops hitting Red and Blue Beaches removed.

In the predawn darkness of September 15, a long column of warships and transports moved up Flying Fish Channel

In the foreground, General Courtney Whitney, General Douglas MacArthur, and Major General Edward Almond watch from on board the U.S.S. *Mt. McKinley* as the shelling on Inchon Harbor begins.

toward Wolmi-do. All the while, Navy shells whistled overhead from the rear and blasted the island. Then, as the column neared its target and the men of the 5th Marines began climbing down from their ships to the landing craft that would carry them ashore, planes swooped in ahead of them on strafing and bombing runs. At 6:25 A.M., the landing craft started toward Wolmi-do.

Eight minutes later, the Marines were charging ashore at the island's northern end, with larger vessels carrying three

Sherman tanks arriving just behind them. Once on land, one unit hurried across the island to take a causeway that extended over to Inchon and then to fend off any North Koreans who might come dashing across from the city. Other units attacked Wolmi-do's main hill.

As the men of one unit moved up its slopes, North Korean soldiers suddenly appeared in front of them, climbing out of foxholes and holding their hands high in surrender. Survivors of the vicious bombardments of the past days, they were exhausted, dazed, and afraid they were going to be killed. They sighed with relief when the Marines sent them back down to the beach under guard.

On another part of the hill, the invaders ran into a group of North Koreans with no thought of surrender. Lurking in foxholes and caves, the enemy soldiers began to fling hand grenades at the oncomers. The Marines dove for cover and opened fire with their rifles and automatic weapons. Soon one of the Sherman tanks rumbled up alongside them. Its nose was fitted with a bulldozer blade and, scooping up great chunks of earth as it went, the tank moved in among the NK defenders. It covered over the foxholes and collapsed the cave openings. The enemy soldiers were buried alive.

On still another section of the hill, the Marines reached the shattered crest and fastened an American flag to the tallest tree stump they could find. It was 7:00 A.M., just thirty minutes since the 5th had landed. By 11:00 A.M. the battle was over, and the island was completely in American hands. The Marines learned that Wolmi-do had more than 400 men left guarding it that morning. Of that number, 180 had been killed, 136 captured, and upwards of 100 buried alive by the bulldozing Sherman. The 5th had suffered 17 men wounded but no fatalities.

The tide had by now crested and receded. The Marines were stranded on their prize, completely surrounded by mud. They could only hope that a North Korean force would not come knifing across the causeway from Inchon before the next high tide brought them reinforcements and the sunset landings at Red and Blue Beaches.

A U.S. Marine stands guard over a band of North Korean prisoners on Wolmi-Do Island. The captives were stripped of their clothes in the search for concealed weapons.

INCHON FALLS

There was no reason to worry. No one appeared on the causeway. Beginning four hours before the landings, the Navy bombarded Red and Blue Beaches and the areas behind them. Planes roared in on strafing and bombing runs. Then, at 5:30 P.M. a fleet of landing craft started plowing up to the two beaches.

Watched by their comrades on Wolmi-do, units of the 5th Marines hit Red Beach. The beach, which extended 300 yards (247 meters) down to the causeway running out to

Wolmi-do, was fronted by a seawall ranging in height from 14 to 16 feet (4 to 5 meters). Behind it lay the heart of Inchon.

The prelanding bombardment had shattered stretches of the seawall. As wave after wave of landing craft arrived, the Marines climbed over the rubble, charged forward, and immediately ran into fire from an enemy entrenchment. They pressed on and uprooted the North Koreans at a cost of eight men killed and twenty-eight wounded. Among the dead was a young officer who was felled by a machine-gun burst as he raised his arm to throw a grenade at an enemy pillbox. He rolled over on the grenade and allowed it to explode under him so that his men would not be hit by flying shrapnel.

Minutes after fighting their way past the entrenchment, the Marines were crowding up the slopes of Cemetery Hill, their first objective. At its crest, they were greeted by North Koreans who threw down their weapons in surrender. So stunned and deafened were they by the afternoon's bombardment that they wanted no part of the fighting.

From Cemetery Hill, the attackers swung south to Observatory Hill, which overlooked the harbor and Wolmi-do. Slowly they worked their way up its 200-foot (61-meter) slopes at sunset, fighting off enemy fire, wiping the wetness of a sudden rain from their eyes, and then squinting through the darkness when night came. At midnight, they stood atop their prize.

On reaching Blue Beach, the lst Marines climbed its seawall and speared quickly inland toward the highway leading to Seoul. They lost one man killed and nineteen wounded in the hours of fighting it took to reach the roadway. Like the troops on Observatory Hill, they had their objective in hand by midnight.

There was sporadic fighting through the rest of the night as the Americans pressed inland among burning buildings from Red and Blue Beaches. At 7:30 A.M. on September 16, the leading troops of the two forces met on the far side of Inchon. In the hours of one rainy night, the city had been completely sealed off. The Americans now turned to their next task: the recapture of Seoul and its return to South Korean hands.

CHAPTER 5

TO THE 38TH PARALLEL AND BEYOND

WITH INCHON BEHIND THEM, the 5th Marines and the 1st Marine Division sped toward Seoul. After a few miles the 5th swung away to attack Kimpo Airfield, while the 1st continued toward the capital.

Kimpo was South Korea's largest airport and lay about 8 miles (13 kilometers) outside Seoul. Blasting aside T34 tanks that loomed in their path, the 5th reached the field in the early evening of September 17, took its southern half, and dug in for the night. They were attacked five times in the next hours by small NK units that had rushed to the aid of the airfield. The 5th repulsed every assault and finally routed the enemy at dawn with a blanket of rocket fire laid down by a battalion newly arrived from Inchon.

Kimpo was completely in Marine hands by midday, September 18. That afternoon, combat planes from Japan began landing at the field. Air strikes were being launched from there by September 20.

OUT FROM THE PUSAN PERIMETER

Far to the south, General Walker began to thrust out of the Pusan Perimeter on September 16. But his men received an ugly surprise when they attacked. There were more North Koreans facing them than they had expected.

MacArthur had thought that the NKs on the Perimeter would immediately rush back to Seoul on hearing of the invasion. But their commander, fearing that word of Inchon would demoralize them, had kept the invasion a secret and had quietly sent just a few units northward. Consequently, when Walker started out of the Perimeter, he came up against most of the 70,000 troops that had been plaguing him for weeks.

His men advanced slowly against stiff resistance for almost a week. Then, as the news of Inchon and the mounting threat to Seoul filtered south, the resistance collapsed. The North Koreans realized that they were about to be trapped between two massive forces, and that they would be without food and ammunition once their supply line from Seoul was cut. They broke away from Walker in a sudden panic, throwing their arms aside and fleeing in any direction that promised safety. Some went into hiding in remote villages. Others faded into the surrounding mountains, there to fight as guerrillas for months to come.

Now, wherever Walker's troops looked, they saw abandoned rifles, ammunition, artillery pieces, vehicles, and equipment littering the roadways. And, wherever they went, they encountered enemy troops ready to surrender. Of the 70,000 North Koreans who had been on the Perimeter at the start of the breakout, only 25,000 to 30,000 completed the northward retreat.

CLOSING IN ON SEOUL

At Inchon, X Corps' 7th Division came ashore on September 18. The infantrymen hurried along a curving route to the

PRESIDENT HARRY S. TRUMAN

Born in Lamar, Missouri, in 1884, Harry S. Truman served in World War I, spent the immediate postwar years in private business, and entered local politics in the early 1920s. He was elected to the United States Senate in 1934 and again in 1940. During World War II, Truman headed a Senate committee charged with investigating military spending. Widely liked for his peppery, plain-spoken ways and for the energetic efforts he gave to his committee work, he was named as Franklin D. Roosevelt's running mate in the President's successful 1944 bid for a fourth term in the White House.

Truman served as Vice President for only a few weeks before Roosevelt's death in April 1945. He began his tenure as the nation's thirty-third President by ordering the atomic bomb attacks on the Japanese cities of Hiroshima and Nagasaki that brought World War II in the Pacific to an end. He then went on to establish the Truman Doctrine, the Marshall Plan, and his Four Point Program for providing assistance to backward areas as a means of preventing the spread of communism. Nationally, he proposed social-welfare programs, fostered early civil-rights efforts, and ordered the desegregation of the U.S. armed forces.

After earning the nation's respect for his decisiveness in coming to South Korea's aid in June 1950, Truman saw his popularity wane as the war dragged on and decided not to run for reelection in 1952. He remained active in politics throughout his retirement years, lectured extensively, helped to found the Truman Library, and wrote three books: *Memoirs* (in two volumes) and *Mr. Citizen*. In those final years, he won back the popularity and admiration that he had lost during the Korean War. He died on December 26, 1972, at age eighty-eight.

giant air base at Suwon, 20 miles (32 kilometers) directly south of Seoul. Their assignment was to capture the base, cut the main supply road to Pusan, and then join the attack on Seoul.

Less than a week after the Inchon landing, Seoul was facing disaster. The 5th Marines were closing in from the northwest. The lst Marine Division, coming directly from the west, was battling its way into the outskirts of the capital. Then, on September 21, the X Corps hit Seoul itself, now turned into a fortress by NK units that had been rushing to its defense since the Inchon landing. The 5th and lst moved in side by side, absorbing heavy losses as they hit one enemy position after another. They were soon joined by a newly arrived outfit, the 7th Marine Regiment, that came spearing in from the northwest. Elements of the 7th Division, accompanied by ROK units, charged north from Suwon. An armored unit of the Eighth Army made contact with the 7th Marines and sealed off the city from the east.

The battle for Seoul raged for more than a week. The attacking troops shot their way into barricaded streets. They fought in burning buildings. To reach the enemy, they climbed over the rubble left by artillery bombardments and air assaults. They struck at T34s and left them burning. They flushed out machine-gun nests and silenced artillery positions with hand grenades and bazookas.

No matter how well the city was defended, there was never a doubt that Seoul would fall to the attackers. In the first days of the war, the Americans had been driven south by a force infinitely larger than theirs. Now the situation was reversed. The North Koreans were being crushed in the jaws of a giant vise formed by the Eighth Army and X Corps. Dazed, the enemy troops were sent tumbling out of the city and back across the 38th Parallel by a mass of men and equipment that they could not match.

By the time the battle was ending, much of Seoul had been reduced to smoking ruins. On September 28, MacArthur flew into Kimpo and drove with President Syng-

Three Marines fight their way through the capital city of Seoul. The portraits on the building are of Josef Stalin, on the left, and Premier Kim Il Sung of North Korea. The Marine on the right has snagged a few ducks for dinner.

man Rhee to the capital's battered Assembly Chamber. There, to the accompaniment of distant artillery fire, the general handed the city back to the aging Rhee in a brief and simple ceremony.

"In behalf of the United Nations Command," MacArthur said, "I am happy to restore to you, Mr. President, the seat of your government that from it you may better fulfill your constitutional responsibilities."

THE NEXT STEP

Even as the Inchon landing was being planned, there had been no doubt of what MacArthur hoped to do once Seoul was his. Enthusiastically supported by Rhee, he wanted to pursue the demoralized NK troops across the 38th Parallel and throughout North Korea, at last totally destroying them and toppling their country's Communist government. Then all of Korea could be reunited under Rhee.

But MacArthur could not order a border crossing on his own. The struggle in South Korea had always been intended as a "police action," meant only to drive out the invaders and restore peace to the nation. To carry the fighting into North Korea would go beyond the boundaries of a "police action." It was a matter that needed to be authorized by President Truman and sanctioned by the United Nations.

The prospect of invading North Korea received a mixed greeting in Washington and caused days of debate. President Truman, the Joint Chiefs of Staff, and most congressional leaders supported the idea. They thought it useless to fight an enemy without completely defeating him. Further, were the North Koreans allowed to hide beyond the Parallel, they would rearm themselves and attack again on some future day. Finally, in light of the opposition to communism shared by millions of Americans, the chance to overthrow North Korea's Communist regime and replace it with a democratic government could not go ignored.

There were, however, dissenting voices. Some officials warned that an attack across the 38th Parallel might well trigger the horror that had concerned the President from the very start of the Korean crisis—a war with China or the Soviet Union, or both—because those nations feared that the attack might be carried into their own territories. China loomed as the country more likely to fight. It would feel especially threatened because its region of Manchuria ran alongside North Korea for several hundred miles, from the Bay of Korea in the southwest to a point near the Sea of Japan in the northeast. It touched the Russian border as it approached the sea.

Truman, however, felt that the risk of war with either country was small. Communist China and Chiang Kai-shek's Nationalist government on Taiwan were snarling at each other across the waters that separated them, with each seeming ready to invade the other. That problem could keep China from jumping into the Korean fight. Also, the Chinese were saddled with massive economic problems after the years of fighting to drive Chiang Kai-shek out and could scarcely afford another war. Finally, U.S. intelligence reports indicated that China had no intention of getting involved in a Korean conflict.

As for the Soviets, Truman and others now thought they were not interested in fighting in Korea. They had never acted to stop the UN from intervening in the war and had allowed representative Jacob Malik to continue boycotting the organization. They seemed content to let the North Koreans fend for themselves.

At the end of September, MacArthur received a communiqué from Truman and the Joint Chiefs that ended the debate. It authorized the advance across the Parallel by telling him that his primary mission was now to destroy all North Korean forces. He was also to unify all Korea under Syngman Rhee, if that were to prove possible. He was to keep an eye on China and the Soviet Union. And he was to inform Washington immediately if either or both gave any sign of joining the fighting.

MacArthur was now free to put into action the strategy he had developed for conquering North Korea. He would split the country between General Walker's Eighth Army and General Almond's X Corps. The Eighth would strike across the Parallel in the west, while X Corps landed at the port of Wonsan on the east coast, some 100 miles (161 kilometers) north of the Parallel. From there, the Corps would advance across North Korea for a meeting with Walker's men. The two forces would then drive the enemy back to the Yalu River, which formed more than 300 miles (483 kilometers) of the Chinese-Korean border. Once the North Koreans were hemmed in against the river, there would be no room left for fighting and the war would be over.

The communiqué, however, placed two restrictions on the general, both meant to calm the fears of the Chinese that the UN forces—especially the Americans—would enter their territory. He was not to send aircraft across the Chinese border and was to allow only the ROK units with Walker and Almond to press close to it. All non-ROK forces were to remain along a line 30 to 40 miles (48 to 64 kilometers) away, so as to avoid a direct confrontation between China and the United States.

Four developments came fast on the heels of the communiqué. On October 1, ROK units opened the first phase of X Corps' attack. They surged across the Parallel and started to drive the enemy up the east coast toward Wonsan. That same day, MacArthur, in a bid to avoid further fighting, demanded that North Korean Premier Kim Il Sung surrender his country; the demand went ignored. Next, on October 3, China issued an ominous warning:

"If the United States or the United Nations forces cross the 38th Parallel, the Chinese People's Republic will send aid to the People's Republic of Korea. We shall not take this action, however, if only South Korean troops cross the border."

Jubilant ROK and UN troops with a sign they will put up along one of the roads that crossed the 38th Parallel.

The third development came on October 7. The United Nations sanctioned the advance into North Korea.

The Chinese announcement triggered a fresh wave of concern in the Washington officials who opposed the crossing. It was known from intelligence sources, they warned, that the Chinese had more than thirty divisions stationed in

Manchuria—far too many for MacArthur to handle if they decided to cause trouble. It was foolhardy to risk a war with the world's most populous country; though equipment was limited, it could supply an almost limitless number of men to the fighting. The general and Syngman Rhee ignored the warning, pointing to the U.S. intelligence sources indicating that China really did not want to intervene.

INTO NORTH KOREA

On October 9, the lst Cavalry Division, accompanied by other UN units, began the Eighth Army's attack northward. They moved out of the town of Kaesong, a short distance north of Seoul, and swept across the Parallel with their eyes on Pyongyang, the North Korean capital. On the east coast, the ROK units moved steadily toward Wonsan. Victories came quickly for the UN troops. Wonsan fell on October 10–11. The lst Cavalry, after breaking through a heavy defense line with British, Australian, and ROK contingents, captured Pyongyang on October 19.

Only one aspect of the invasion went wrong. Almond's X Corps had to send its lst Marine Division and 7th Division sailing around Korea from Inchon to the east coast so that they could join the ROKs in the push inland from Wonsan. The journey was plagued by a variety of problems, and the lst Marines did not reach Wonsan until more than two weeks after the port had fallen, with the 7th going ashore at Iwon farther up the coast.

Despite X Corps' problems, the UN advances were made so swiftly that it was a highly confident MacArthur who greeted Truman when the two held a meeting on Wake Island on October 15 to discuss the war. The President was worried about the possibility of Chinese intervention and had sent word through UN channels to assure the Communist Chinese government that the United States had no designs on China. General MacArthur reported that all was going so

taking Pyongyang, Walker's Eighth Army sent its American, British, Australian, and ROK troops marching out of the North Korean capital. Fighting a tattered NK army, they quickly advanced to their next target, the Chongchon River, 45 miles (72 kilometers) away. The river flowed out of central North Korea and crossed their path as it ran to the Yellow Sea. It flowed in the same southeasterly direction as the Yalu River, about 60 miles (96 kilometers) farther north. Once the Chongchon was reached, the men of the Eighth would begin their push toward the Yalu and final victory.

On the east coast, X Corps' ROK troops were moving north from Wonsan, while the lst Marine and 7th Divisions were preparing to come ashore—the lst at Wonsan and the 7th at Iwon farther north. Both would then plunge inland. The Marines would climb to the vast 4,000-foot (1,219-meter) plateau where they would find the Changjin-Chosin reservoir. In the bitter winter ahead, it would become known to all Americans as the Chosin reservoir. From there, they were to press on and join the Eighth Army for the assault on the Yalu.

MacARTHUR CHANGES THE RULES

On October 24, still in the dark about the CCF presence, MacArthur passed a new instruction to his field commanders. No longer were they to heed the Joint Chiefs' stipulation that only ROK troops were to approach the Chinese border and that all non-ROK troops were to remain well behind. Now that the Eighth was nearing the limit set by the Chiefs, all UN forces—ROK and non-ROK alike—were to speed to the border and win the war as soon as possible.

The Joint Chiefs were furious when they learned of the general's action. This was sheer disobedience. It was a direct violation of an order meant to keep the United States and China from confronting each other directly and igniting a full-scale war. President Truman must have been angered, too, though he did not publicly say so. MacArthur's action drove a wedge between the two men, a wedge that would cut too deeply in 1951.

The general's new order accelerated the advances toward the Yalu. After crossing the Chongchon River, some Eighth Army units moved west and others continued north. The 2nd Division, thrusting west, fought to within 18 miles (29 kilometers) of the Yalu near the river's entry into the Yellow Sea. ROK units to the north approached the city of Chosan on the Yalu; it was to be the point farthest north reached by the United Nations Command. Both were turned back after October 25. That was the day the UN troops met the Chinese.

FIRST CONTACTS WITH THE CHINESE

That meeting took place soon after a ROK regiment had passed through the town of Unsan north of the Chongchon. Suddenly, the South Koreans threw themselves to the ground as mortar shells came hurtling in on them. In the brief but fierce skirmish that followed, they sighted 300 enemy soldiers and captured a prisoner.

The regimental officers were shocked when they found that, though he was wearing a North Korean uniform (as did many of the CCF soldiers) the prisoner could not speak Korean but was fluent in Chinese. They rushed him off to the Eighth Army's advance headquarters for further questioning. There he completely baffled his interrogators. Was he a member of a Chinese volunteer company that had joined the NK army? Or had a Chinese force somehow slipped over the border without being sighted?

The puzzle began to unravel in the next days. Three more Chinese were taken prisoner in attacks that were aimed chiefly at South Korean units. On the eastern front, troops identified as being with the CCF hit and annihilated a ROK unit. On the western front, the Chinese snapped shut a trap that cost a ROK regiment 350 men, either killed or wounded. In another encounter, a fellow regiment lost all but 875 of its 3,500 men.

When the Eighth Army's 24th Division came to within 18 miles (29 kilometers) of the Yalu, its men captured a number of Chinese after advancing in the face of an especially fierce resistance. General Walker had thought that the 24th had been battling with NK units. The fierce resistance had struck him as odd because most of the North Korean troops, discouraged and battered, had not often put up strong fights. But now he became convinced that the division was facing not an unusually stubborn NK foe but a major Chinese force. For safety's sake, he ordered the 24th back to the Chong-chon River, there to set up a strong defensive line and await further orders.

This group of soldiers was among the first of the Chinese troops to be captured as prisoners of war.

By the end of October, the CCF units were no longer concentrating on the ROKs. They were hitting troops of every kind on both the western and eastern fronts. They would suddenly burst from cover in their *Hachi-Shiki* formation—a V formation with the open end of the V facing the enemy. The V would fan out in two arcs that then curled in behind the enemy. With their prey encircled, the Chinese would throw in wave after wave of men, do as much damage as possible, and vanish. Left dead in the wake of one attack were 600 Americans. They gave added proof to what the U.S. field commanders were now suspecting: that there weren't just a few Chinese volunteer units in North Korea but at least several divisions.

The attacks continued into November, when the first snows of winter began to fall. Then, on November 6, just as suddenly as they had begun, the attacks ended. UN planes and ground patrols went searching for CCF camps. Not one was sighted. For some reason, the Chinese had disappeared into the North Korean forests or back across the border to Manchuria. Everywhere, all was quiet. MacArthur and the troops could only wonder if the quiet marked the end of China's intervention in the war. Or was it only a lull in the fighting? No one could say.

(The reason for the disappearance remains a mystery to this day. A popular theory holds that the Chinese joined the war to warn the United Nations of the fighting to come if Manchuria was attacked, and then vanished to give the UN time to reconsider MacArthur's drive north and order it to be called off.)

THE BRIDGES ACROSS THE YALU

When the CCF attacks began, MacArthur refused to believe that China had released a major force into North Korea. At first, he claimed there were no Chinese at all in front of him. Next, with mounting evidence of the Chinese presence, he insisted that the newcomers must be members of a few volunteer units; they were meant to do nothing but hamper the advances to the Yalu River. But by the dawn of November, with the attacks hitting at so many points and with his field commanders saying that entire Chinese divisions were in Korea, MacArthur was forced to a complete change of mind. It was a change that came painfully. He hated to admit that an enemy was out there who could stop his advance on the Yalu and keep him from the final—the crowning—victory of his career.

Helping convince him was information that he received on November 1. UN pilots reported seeing Chinese troops moving south at night across the twelve highway and railroad bridges that spanned the Yalu to link Manchuria with Korea. This was a danger that could not be ignored. The general ordered B-29s to bomb the bridges the next day and informed the Joint Chiefs of his decision. They replied with an order that sent him into a fury.

In keeping with President Truman's word that the United States would not strike into China, the bridges were not to be bombed until the matter could be studied further. Nor were any targets within 5 miles (8 kilometers) of the river to be hit; these targets included electrical plants that provided power to Manchuria and the USSR's Siberia. The enraged general fired off an angry message to the Joint Chiefs, telling them that he would obey their order but that his men would soon face disaster if the bridges were not taken out. The flood of incoming Chinese had to be stopped.

The message stunned the Chiefs. MacArthur's earlier communiqués had downplayed the Chinese threat. But now he was predicting doom for his men. Why this abrupt switch? Were new Chinese troops coming into the field in force? Or had he been downplaying the Chinese threat so that, in the name of avoiding a war with China, he would not be ordered to stop his advances and be cheated of the final victory he so desperately wanted?

The troubled Chiefs went to President Truman for a decision on the problem—a decision that he made on the basis that his chief commander believed the bombings were necessary while the Joint Chiefs could think of no alternative action to put in their stead. As a result, MacArthur received word that the bridges could be bombed, but only out to their mid-spans, the point at which the Chinese-Korean border was drawn.

This was an obvious attempt to protect the UN troops and China's territory all at the same time. But it only fed MacArthur's anger. It was silly to expect the B-29s to hit the bridges only on one side. Because of antiaircraft guns that the Chinese had placed along the river, the bombers would have to attack from 18,000 feet (5,486 meters), where they would be tossed about by fierce winds. Accuracy would be impossible. Chinese territory was sure to be hit.

Nevertheless, the bombings began, with the pilots returning with news that caused the irate general to take another step. He informed the Chiefs that enemy planes— Russian MIGs obviously flown by Chinese pilots—were now streaking out of Manchuria, attacking his bombers, and then escaping to safety back over the border. He asked that UN fighters be given an extra chance to down the enemy aircraft by chasing them into Manchuria for three minutes of flying time. The request was based on the old rule of "hot pursuit." Long established in international law, the rule stemmed from the ancient principle that gave the police, when "hotly" pursuing a felon, the right to carry their chase beyond the boundaries of their jurisdiction.

The request created a new problem for Truman and the Joint Chiefs. The United States had recently promised to confer with its UN allies in Korea before allowing MacArthur to take any action threatening Manchuria. They now turned down the general's request, fearing that any violation of Manchurian airspace would bring on retaliatory strikes by both the Chinese and Soviets and possibly trigger a third world war.

The bombings continued until mid-December and were seen as a failure; of the twelve bridges, only four were disabled. Left behind by the argument over them were deep scars. MacArthur continued to brand the order to bomb the spans only on their Korean sides and to refrain from hitting the electric plants that gave aid to the enemy as being the most foolish ever handed to a commander. How could he win a war with his hands tied behind his back for political reasons? Though his words were aimed at the Joint Chiefs, they also reflected on Truman's leadership in the war. The wedge between the two men was driven deeper.

THE FINAL CAMPAIGN

Just as the arguments over the bridges left scars, so did the CCF disappearance on November 6 leave behind all the questions of what had happened to the Chinese, where they had gone, and why they had vanished. Whatever the answers might be, MacArthur decided to spend the next weeks resting his troops and supplying them with fresh arms and equipment. Then, on November 24, he would unleash his final campaign against the Yalu. The Eighth Army would lunge forward from the Chongchon River. X Corps' lst Marine Division was at the Chosin reservoir and would push off from there to link up with the Eighth for the final thrust to the Yalu.

To raise troop morale, MacArthur visited the Eighth Army's front and told one of his commanders that he hoped the campaign would be successful and bring "the boys home by Christmas." The press picked up the remark and flashed it to the world. The new campaign was quickly dubbed the "Win-the-War Offensive" or the "Home-for-Christmas Drive."

It was to fail to live up to either name.

Responsible for that failure would be an aging Chinese soldier—General Peng De-huai, the commander of the Chinese forces in North Korea. He had let his men hide in the forests long enough. He was ready to fight again.

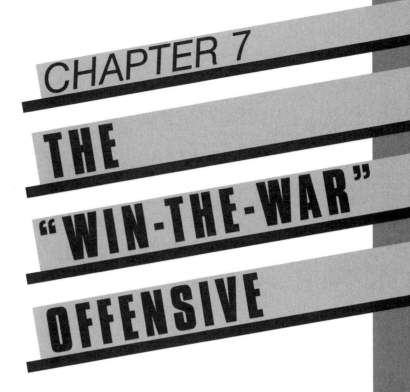

CHAPTER 7

THE "WIN-THE-WAR" OFFENSIVE

AT THE TIME OF THE "Win-the-War" offensive, General Peng was commanding 300,000 Chinese troops (plus perhaps 40,000 North Koreans). The Chinese were divided into two giant forces, with 180,000 men facing the Eighth Army in the west and 120,000 waiting for X Corps in the east. Due to battle the two were 247,000 United Nations troops. In all, the UN troops were outnumbered by at least 53,000 men.

Peng was planning a two-pronged strategy for victory. First, he would prevent a linkup of the Eighth Army and X Corps. To do this, he would hit the right side of Walker's army and seal off the gap that extended over to the X Corps front at the Chosin reservoir. Then he would set North Korea free by driving the enemy into the sea—the Eighth Army back over the 38th Parallel and into the Yellow Sea, and X Corps eastward into the Sea of Japan.

THE "WIN-THE-WAR" OFFENSIVE IN THE WEST

As scheduled, General Walker opened the offensive in the west on November 24. His Eighth Army now consisted of four U.S. divisions, four ROK divisions, and two brigades—one Turkish and the other British. With the exception of the 1st Cavalry Division, which he held in reserve, his troops crossed a broad stretch of the Chongchon River and moved toward the Yalu River along ice-slick roads and over snow-covered hills, with all going well until the night of November 25.

It was then that the CCF hit Walker's right flank, where three of his four ROK divisions were advancing. Suddenly, hordes of Chinese came bursting out of the darkness, filling the icy air with the sounds of screeching whistles, blaring trumpets, and clanging gongs. The racket frightened the South Koreans, though it was not intended as a "scare tactic." The various sounds were used as signals for positioning and moving the attacking troops.

The fear created by the din was a bonus. For the ROKs, it triggered the memory of the terrible beatings they had taken at the hands of the CCF in October and early November. They panicked as the enemy rolled over them in waves. They broke and began to flee south.

Walker quickly ordered the 1st Cavalry in from its reserve position to stop the attack. At the same time, he pulled the British and Turkish brigades from the center of his line to help. But there were simply too many Chinese to handle. No one could stop them. They soon had Walker completely cut off from X Corps.

In the meantime, swarms of Chinese struck all along the general's front. In the next two days, his troops were swept back across the Chongchon. At the same time, the Chinese who had flooded through the gap were curling in behind him. By November 28, knowing that his men had but one chance to avoid being entrapped and slaughtered, he ordered a retreat. He took his army, with the Chinese close behind, reeling down to the area around Pyongyang.

The job of protecting the retreat went to the 2nd Division. The rearguard action took the division back across the Chongchon at several points, with some units reaching a spot 7 miles (11 kilometers) from Sunchon, a town now held by the 1st Cavalry.

At month's end, these units—totaling 7,000 men—formed a column of trucks, jeeps, and artillery for the run along a dirt road to Sunchon. No sooner had they started than they found that the road was held by the enemy.

Positioned at points on both sides of the road were Chinese mortar, machine-gun, and sniper posts. As the column pressed forward, it was repeatedly caught in a deadly crossfire. Vehicles would slam to a halt. Men would jump to the ground and return the fire. The fighting would continue until UN planes swept in to strafe and bomb the enemy positions, either wiping them out or sending their troops running to safety. Then the artillery, trucks, and jeeps, with soldiers pushing aside the burning or wrecked vehicles, would inch forward once again.

Night brought a new danger. Now the column was hit not only from the sides but also from the rear. Chinese soldiers flooded onto the road to Sunchon behind the last of the trucks and constantly attacked them with rifles, bayonets, and hand grenades.

But, at last, the column broke free of the Chinese crossfire and rolled into Sunchon and the temporary safety it offered. It took three days for the 7,000 men to "run the gauntlet" and cost them 4,000 comrades killed and wounded, plus huge losses in vehicles and equipment.

The 2nd Division and the 1st Cavalry now moved south to the defensive line at Pyongyang. It failed to hold when the Chinese smashed through its center and sent Walker stumbling back across the 38th Parallel.

By mid-December, a mere three weeks after he had launched MacArthur's "Win-the-War" offensive in the west, General Walker's troops were taking up defensive positions north and east of Seoul.

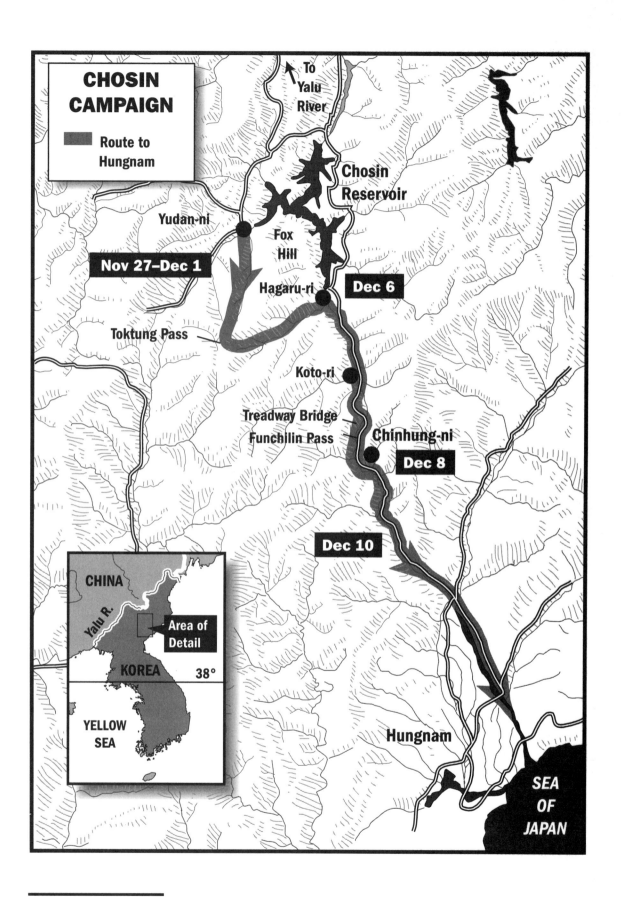

THE "WIN-THE-WAR" OFFENSIVE IN THE EAST

X Corps also opened the offensive on November 24. By then, the lst Marine Division and elements of the 7th Infantry Division were at the Chosin reservoir. The great bulk of the 7th had returned to the coast to join other units (among them the ROK outfits that had earlier captured Wonsan) in guarding the port city of Hungnam. Located north of Wonsan, the port was serving as the supply base for X Corps because it stood at the foot of the 78-mile (126-kilometer) road up to the reservoir.

On arriving at Chosin in the days before November 24, General Oliver Smith, the commander of the lst Marines, stationed his men at points around and below the reservoir. Marines were entrenched near the village of Yudam-ni on its west bank. Units of the 7th dotted the east bank. Other Marines were at Hagaru-ri at the reservoir's southern tip. Still others were stationed at Koto-ri and Chinhung-ni some miles down the road to Hungnam.

Because of its location, Hagaru-ri became Smith's headquarters. It was the scene of feverish activity in the days before the offensive opened. Troops and supplies arrived daily. A hospital and supply depot took shape. Engineers worked day and night in below-zero temperatures to build an airfield for C-47 cargo planes so that supplies could be brought in more quickly from the coast.

As new troops arrived, Smith sent them over to Yudam. It was to be the springboard for his thrust westward. But the idea of the move troubled him. While advancing on Chosin, his men had been repeatedly attacked by CCF units. He suspected, correctly, that a giant Chinese force was lurking in the snows around the reservoir. His Marines at Yudam would be heavily outnumbered when they moved west. He told them to advance slowly and cautiously.

On the first day of the offensive, the Marines advanced into the hills in front of Yudam and, on November 27, found out how right Smith had been. They were hit by withering

THE WAR IN THE AIR AND AT SEA

From the very beginning of the war, the United Nations Command received heavy air support—so heavy that the UN planes soon established air superiority over all of Korea. They held that superiority throughout the fighting, even when faced with the 2,500 aircraft (mostly Russian-built MIGs) that the Chinese sent against them.

The air support began in June 1950 with President Truman's order that U.S. warplanes cover the evacuation of foreign nationals from beleaguered Seoul and protect the first war supplies being sent to Korea from depots in Japan. By late June 1953, three years later, United Nations warplanes of all types—taking off from bases in Japan, Okinawa, and Korea itself, and from carriers offshore—had flown more than 800,000 sorties and had recorded some 180,000 casualties. Their prime targets included troops, tanks, artillery positions, communication and transportation centers, supply depots, and railroad lines. The railroad attacks were meant to force the enemy to move supplies by trucks, which were then strafed and bombed.

The first jet air battle in history took place over Korea, when an American F-80 met and downed an enemy MIG on November 9, 1950.

In addition to hundreds of landing craft, supply vessels, mine sweepers, and transports that served in the war, approximately 108 warships saw duty in Korean waters: four battleships, eight cruisers, eighty destroyers, and sixteen carriers. Of the carriers, thirteen came from the United States, two from Britain, and one from Australia.

In the course of the fighting, the battleships, cruisers, and destroyers unleashed more than 4 million shells of varying sizes at enemy targets, while Navy and Marine pilots flew more than 225,000 sorties from carrier decks.

Though most of the warships were provided by America, ten other United Nations members placed ships under the command of the U.S. Navy. The largest naval forces of the war were collected for the Inchon invasion and the evacuation from Hungnam, with the former being the greatest assemblage of ships and landing craft since the invasion of Okinawa in World War II.

Brought to a high level of heroic performance and success during the Korean fighting were the helicopter efforts to rescue downed pilots and troopers. "Choppers" plucked the soldiers from the sea or flew in to snatch them up from behind enemy lines.

gunfire, fought back for as long as possible, and then withdrew to set up a strong defensive perimeter around Yudam.

For the next two days, in temperatures that blackened them with frostbite and froze many of their weapons, the Marines fought off CCF attacks all along the perimeter. But they were not the only ones in battle. The Chinese also struck the 7th Division units on the eastern bank, trapping them until rescuers came up from Hagaru-ri. That village, too, was hit, as were points along the Hungnam road.

Smith was commanding 20,000 men and, by November 30, he knew that, like the UN force in the west, they were facing an enemy of impossible size. The Chinese were all around the reservoir and all along the road to Hungnam. If he remained in place, his troops would be annihilated. He had no choice but to send them battling their way back to the coast.

Before starting south, he ordered the Marines at Yudam to Hagaru-ri. Struggling through deep snowdrifts and fighting off the Chinese, the Marines took four days to reach the village, with the last of their number arriving on December 3.

While Smith prepared for the march, Air Force and Marine C-47s flew into Hagaru-ri's airstrip time after time and took aboard the wounded and frostbitten from the village hospital. In five days, the planes removed 4,312 patients to safety.

The general planned to make the march in three stages: first from Hagaru-ri to the American-held village of Koto 11 miles (18 kilometers) away, and then 10 miles on to Chinhung.

It is two days before Christmas in 1950. These men, who have been fighting the Chinese, are happy to take a break by the roadside, snow and all.

At Chinhung, he would be met by 7th Division elements and other units that had come up from Hungnam; they would escort his men on the third and final leg to the coast. Throughout the journey, the marchers would be guarded against the Chinese by an armada of Air Force, Marine, and Navy warplanes, with the Navy planes coming from seven carriers that had gathered offshore near Hungnam.

Early on December 6, a column of trucks, jeeps, tanks, and artillery moved out of Hagaru-ri and soon stretched for miles along the road to Koto. Blinded by a dense fog, Marine units ranged through the hills on either side of the road in search of CCF positions. The column lurched to the first of many stops when heavy enemy fire hit it from somewhere in the hills a short distance from Hagaru-ri. It remained at a standstill until the fog cleared and enabled Marine planes to sight the CCF position and destroy it. At another point, gunfire from a hillside entrenchment stopped all movement. A Marine unit, backed by a tank, cleared the entrenchment. And so, fighting off the enemy as they went, the Americans plodded ahead through the day and night.

The column pulled into Koto on December 7. The next day, in the company of the troops that had been holding Koto, it started along the 10-mile (16-kilometer) run to Chinhung. This was to be the most perilous leg of the journey because it took the vehicles up into the Funchilin Pass. The road through the pass snaked along a steep mountainside and was no more than a single lane wide. If hit by a major attack, the column would have no room to swing around and retreat. It would have to keep moving at all costs.

The trip lived up to its promise of danger. As the column plowed forward, Marine units spread through the hills above Funchilin Pass. The Chinese had planted the hills with strong entrenchments, knowing that if the column got through the pass, they would have little chance of keeping it from reaching Chinhung, where Americans units from the coast waited to help it on to Hungnam. And so, moving blindly through a snowstorm, the Marines had to fight their way from one CCF stronghold to the next. By late afternoon, they took what they thought to be the highest of the hills. They spent the night sitting on their prize, only to have the weather clear and let the dawn show them that they had yet a higher peak to take. Supported by mortar fire and a strike by four Marine planes, they attacked. The peak was theirs by the afternoon.

As the Marines were fighting for the peak, the column braked to halt in the pass. Ahead, the road ended at a yawning chasm and began again on the far side. A bridge had once spanned the chasm but had been blown up by the Chinese. This new obstacle came as no surprise to the Americans. A few days earlier, they had learned about the bridge and had called for sections of a portable bridge to be air-dropped at Koto. Engineers had then carried the sections up to the pass. Now, hugging the mountainside, they wrestled the sections into place.

Once their work was completed—and with the Marines dominating the heights above—the column surged across the new span and hurried on to Chinhung. Then it rumbled past the last CCF positions and entered Hungnam on December 11. There—protected by a ring of tanks and clouds of aircraft—the troops, their vehicles, and their equipment were placed aboard 192 ships that had gathered in the harbor and that would now carry them back across the 38th Parallel.

■■■■■■

The "Win-the-War" offensive was over. For both MacArthur and General Peng, it had been a combined victory and defeat.

Peng had succeeded in hurling the UN troops back over the 38th Parallel. But he had failed to drive them into the sea and rid North Korea of them for good. Both the Eighth Army and X Corps were still intact and ready to fight again.

As for MacArthur, he had suffered the humiliation of seeing his troops surrender all the ground they had won since taking Seoul. But, in fighting as they retreated, both the Eighth Army and X Corps had taken their toll of enemy lives.

On the western front, the Chinese had sustained five times the losses of the UN troops. During the march out of Chosin on the eastern front, General Smith had insisted that his troops were not retreating but "attacking in a new direction." And, indeed, they had attacked, costing the CCF 37,500 casualties compared with 7,500 casualties of their own. Further, they had saved 17,500 vehicles and 350,000 tons of equipment from falling into Peng's hands. In all, the U.S. Navy carried 105,000 troops—and 91,000 North Korean civilians and soldiers who were fleeing the Chinese—away from Hungnam and to safety.

The war was due to continue, but now it was to be a totally different kind of war.

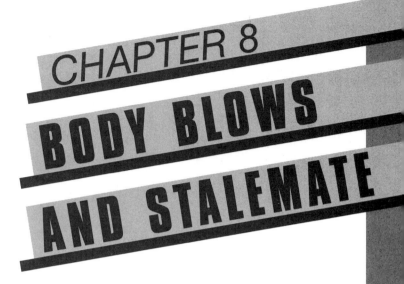

CHAPTER 8

BODY BLOWS AND STALEMATE

IN 1950 THE WAR HAD RAGED from Pusan in the far south to the Chosin reservoir in the north. Now, in 1951, it turned into a slugfest along the 38th Parallel, with the opponents trading blows as though they were heavyweight fighters doing battle in the center of the ring.

BODY BLOWS

As the new year dawned, General Peng struck the Eighth Army's line in the Seoul area and recaptured the capital on January 4. He continued punching southward until the Eighth stopped him 75 miles (121 kilometers) below the city. This was as far as the UN troops would retreat for the rest of the war. They refused to budge in the face of Peng's assaults.

The Eighth fought throughout January under a new commander—Lieutenant General Matthew B. Ridgway, an airborne hero of World War II. The Joint Chiefs gave him the job after General Walker was killed on December 23, when his jeep collided with a ROK truck near the Parallel.

This scene repeated itself many, many times during the war. As the military moved in to push the front forward, civilians in fear for their lives packed what belongings they had and moved out.

Ridgway spent his first weeks in Korea rearming his new troops. Then, on January 24, he launched an attack all along their front, which now extended across the width of the Korean peninsula. They pressed north against a stubborn enemy in February, recaptured Seoul in March, and crossed the 38th Parallel in April. Some miles later, the advance slowed as the attackers took the time to consolidate their gains. Spring was at hand, and they were expecting a major Peng offensive any day now.

It came on April 25. But in the meantime...

THE BEGINNING SEARCH FOR PEACE

In America, the official attitude toward the fighting changed with the failure of the "Win-the-War" offensive. The Truman administration and the United Nations now recognized a cold fact: Victory was not to be won quickly. The Yalu would not be reached and the Chinese driven out of Korea without an awful toll in lives and money. A way had to be found to end the conflict peacefully through talks with the enemy.

MacArthur's failed offensive was not the only reason for the change of attitude. The war was being increasingly criticized throughout the world. The UN had long heard such criticism, but now the outcry was greater than ever. From the start, most of the UN countries had deplored the war, with only fifteen of the organization's sixty members joining the United States in the struggle. The rest had stayed away for reasons ranging from antiwar policies to the fear that it would trigger a greater war.

In the United States, however, the mounting criticism was new. Great segments of the public had originally seen Truman's defense of South Korea as a noble cause. But that nobility had been lost in the grim realities of war. Thousands of men, many of whom had fought in World War II, were being torn from their homes and jobs as reserve and National Guard units were called to active duty. Other thousands were being drafted into the service. Daily, the country had to endure the press reports of soldiers dying or being maimed in battle.

And, daily, the nation felt the economic pinch that accompanies any war. Taxes were increased to pay its costs. Consumer goods made from materials needed for the war effort became scarce. Controls to freeze wages and prices to offset the dangers of wartime inflation were set.

Worst of all, the failed offensive had shattered the dream of a war quickly won. Millions were now asking: How long must our men go on fighting and losing their lives? Why are they fighting someone else's war? Why are they sacrificing themselves in a faraway backwater country?

Clearly, something had to be done to end the fighting quickly and peacefully. The President began to prepare an announcement that he hoped would do just that. He planned to say that, on behalf of the United Nations, he was willing to meet with China and North Korea in an effort to settle the conflict. He would point out that the warring sides had not gained a thing in the months of fighting. There would be no charges of blame or talk of punishment—simply an effort to end the fighting with an armistice that would open the way to a future peace agreement.

The announcement was meant to be a mighty American step along the road to peace. But Truman never had the chance to speak. He was suddenly tripped up by Douglas MacArthur.

TRUMAN DISMISSES MacARTHUR

On March 20, MacArthur received word of Truman's plan. Without a warning to Washington, he broadcast a statement of his own to the enemy. It was a belligerent message in which he warned the Chinese that they were doomed to defeat if the war spread to their country. They had neither the arms nor the equipment necessary to wage a modern war.

He then stated that, as commander of the UN forces, he stood ready to meet with the enemy to find a means of realizing the political aims of the United Nations and thus ending the war.

The message infuriated Truman. The offer to meet with the enemy and "find a means of realizing the political aims of the United Nations" added up to an ultimatum: We'll meet and you'll agree to what we want. In issuing the ultimatum, MacArthur had overstepped his bounds as a military commander. The power to issue ultimatums to the enemy belonged to the President.

(Actually, the general had demanded North Korea's surrender in October 1950, just before moving across the 38th Parallel, but no objections had come from Washington because China was not then involved in the fighting.)

MacArthur had long been driving a wedge between himself and Truman. He had balked at all the U.S. efforts to stay clear of Chinese territory—the orders to keep non-ROK troops well away from the Manchurian border and to avoid bombing the Chinese side of the Yalu bridges. Now he was saying that these political restrictions had kept him from reaching the Yalu and that the war could not be won unless he crossed into China; otherwise, in the safety of Manchuria, the Chinese would rearm themselves for future attacks. Further, as he had done since early in the war, he was advising that Chiang Kai-shek—so hated in Communist China—be allowed to add his troops to the UN Command.

In all, the general wanted nothing less than a complete victory over the Chinese and North Koreans, no matter the cost. It was the view of a soldier who always saw victory as the ultimate goal and who despised the presence of politics in a war.

MacArthur's stance was bad enough for a President who wanted to avoid a full-scale war. But now his ultimatum had driven the wedge too deep. He had not only usurped a presidential power but had also thrown the United Nations—and the world—into confusion. Echoing everywhere was the question: Who in America is actually running the war?

The general had made the nation look like a rudderless ship, and Truman could not release his own announcement for fear of adding to the confusion. The President felt there was only one way for him to regain the world's confidence. He had to prove that, as had always been the case in America, the military was under civilian control and not vice versa.

And so, charging MacArthur with insubordination, he removed him from his command on April 11, 1951.

The news of the removal shocked the world. MacArthur had long been a towering military figure, and many people

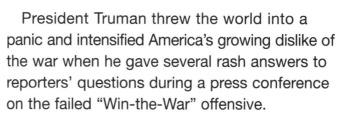

AN ATOMIC BOMB FOR KOREA?

President Truman threw the world into a panic and intensified America's growing dislike of the war when he gave several rash answers to reporters' questions during a press conference on the failed "Win-the-War" offensive.

The conference, which was held in early December 1950, began harmlessly with a formal statement by the President. He said:

> We may suffer reverses as we have suffered them before. But the forces of the United Nations have no intention of abandoning their mission in Korea....

> We shall continue to work in the United Nations for concerted action to halt this aggression in Korea. We shall intensify our efforts to help other free nations strengthen their defenses in order to meet the threat of aggression elsewhere. We shall rapidly increase our military strength.

It was a carefully worded statement that made clear America's determination to continue opposing aggression everywhere. But it caused the reporters to ask just how strongly the United States meant to carry on the fighting in Korea. Mr. Truman answered, "We will take whatever steps are necessary to meet the military situation, just as we always have."

Then came the question that got him into trouble. Would those steps include the use of the atomic bomb? He answered without hesitation, "That includes every weapon we have."

Now Mr. Truman was asked if he meant that the U.S. government was actively considering the use of the atomic bomb in Korea. The President answered: "There has always been active consideration of its use."

It was a rash statement made by a President who was deeply worried about the major defeat his country had just suffered and who was feeling pressured by the questions. It sent a wave of shock and fright rolling across the world. The idea that America might one day unleash a nuclear bomb in Korea if the war could not be won in any other way terrified people everywhere. Remembering how the A-bomb had reduced Japan's Hiroshima and Nagasaki to ashes, people could now envision a nuclear war between the United States and Russia that would turn the planet into a barren wasteland.

The White House was flooded with telephone calls from concerned and angry Americans in the next days. Newspapers in every nation gave the President's answers front-page coverage and brought a storm of protest and criticism. The British government was so troubled that Prime Minister Clement Atlee hurried to Washington to urge that Truman not use the atomic bomb without first consulting Great Britain. The President agreed with the idea, but refused to commit his agreement to writing. He told Atlee that if a man's word wasn't any good it would not be made better by putting it on paper.

In the end, the furor came to nothing. The United States did not use the atomic bomb in Korea and, in the view of many historians, never intended to.

thought it impossible that he should ever be dismissed. He returned home to a hero's welcome—greeted by adoring crowds wherever he went—spoke before a joint session of Congress, and closed his forty-eight-year career with an address to the cadets at West Point. He lived in retirement until his death in 1964, at age eighty-four.

Truman was criticized throughout the nation for the dismissal. One Senator called for his impeachment, another (future President Richard M. Nixon) demanded that MacArthur be returned to his command, and a Gallup Poll showed that the public supported MacArthur over the President by a margin of 69 to 29 percent. In May, however, joint hearings by Senate and House committees looked at the President's action coolly and logically and started the nation on the way to seeing that his decision had been dictated by reason and had upheld the basic American principle of civilian authority over the military.

FIGHTING TO A STALEMATE

On MacArthur's removal, General Ridgway was given the command of the United Nations forces. The Eighth Army went to Lieutenant General James Van Fleet, who had led the initial assault on Utah Beach during the D-Day landings at Normandy, France, in World War II.

By the time Van Fleet took command, the Eighth had increased in size. It now consisted of its old divisions, X Corps, and ROK and other units—in all, a force of just over 580,000 men. Of that number, 229,000 were Americans who had changed much in the months since the first of their number had battled the North Korean thrust toward Pusan. They were no longer inadequately trained raw recruits. They had become experienced veterans, well armed and magnificently backed by air and artillery support.

Soon after Ridgway and Van Fleet took their new posts, the UN forces and the Chinese–North Koreans began trading a series of vicious blows along the Parallel. General Peng struck first when, on April 22, he threw his 700,000-man army against the entire UN front. Most of his troops, however, attacked the western end of the line, their aim being to retake Seoul. Van Fleet retreated as the Chinese pressed toward the city but pounded them relentlessly with air and artillery bombardments. When, as he expected, the attack began to slow, he hit back and stopped the drive 5 miles (8 kilometers) short of its goal.

In May, Peng smashed into the center of the front and forced the defenders into a 12-mile (19-kilometer) retreat. Once again, UN artillery and air power played a major role in ending the assault. The artillery bombardments, nicknamed "Van Fleet's Load," were especially lethal, expending five times the number of shells usually loosed in battle. One artillery battalion fired 12,000 shells in a single day. When the attack began to stumble, Van Fleet again counterpunched. The enemy reeled back across the 38th Parallel.

By June 1951, the UN front line angled across Korea from a point some 40 miles (64 kilometers) north of the Parallel in

Victorious American troops take their positions atop the infamous Heartbreak Ridge. As this photograph shows, the battle was as devastating to the landscape as it was to human life.

the east to a point a few miles below it in the far west. The fighting was just a year old. In that time, the UN forces had inflicted 600,000 casualties on the North Koreans, and more than 500,000 on the CCF. Both sides now dug in on the hills along that front and spent the rest of 1951 and all of 1952 in small but vicious attacks to gain a little ground here and there and improve their positions. The sites of these miniature mountain battles gave the world such memorable names as Heartbreak Ridge and Old Baldy. Then, in 1952, with the Chinese bringing more cannon into play, the attacks were joined by an unending series of deadly artillery duels. The war had become stalemated.

Why? Because the talk of peace had been revived and both sides were waiting for it to bear fruit.

CHAPTER 9

THE STRUGGLE
FOR PEACE

THERE WAS NEW TALK OF PEACE, but quiet was not to come to Korea without a struggle. That struggle began on June 23, 1951, almost exactly a year after the war had erupted and three months after MacArthur had sabotaged Truman's peace offer. On that day, Jacob Malik, the Soviet delegate to the United Nations, spoke before the Security Council. He was no longer boycotting the UN and he advised that: ". . . discussions should be started between the belligerents for a cease-fire and an armistice providing for the mutual withdrawal of forces from the 38th Parallel."

Coming from the representative of the power that Truman suspected was behind the North Korean invasion, the advice was astonishing. It indicated to Truman that the Soviets were as tired of the war as were the UN and America. He immediately instructed Ridgway to arrange the armistice negotiations. The general communicated with General Peng and North Korean Premier Kim Il Sung and suggested that they meet with his representatives on neutral "ground"—namely, aboard a Danish hospital ship in Wonsan harbor—to lay plans for the talks. China balked at the idea and proposed that the town of Kaesong, 3 miles (5 kilometers) south of the

General George C. Marshall

During World War II, General Marshall directed U.S. military operations in both Europe and the Pacific. President Truman named him secretary of state in 1947, a position that Marshall held until illness forced him to retire in 1949. In 1950, however, he returned to government service as secretary of defense, retiring for a final time in 1951. In 1953 he was awarded the Nobel Peace Prize for his development of the Marshall Plan.

General Omar Bradley

During World War II, General Bradley led the U.S. forces in the invasions of North Africa, Sicily, and Normandy. He continued to lead them in the drive across France and into Germany. He served as chairman of the Joint Chiefs of Staff from 1949 to 1953 and, along with General Marshall, supported President Truman's dismissal of MacArthur in 1951.

General Bradley retired from military service in 1953.

Lieutenant General Walton Walker

The commander of the Eighth Army until his death in a jeep accident in December 1950, General Walker was known to his friends as "Johnny" and had the reputation of being a fast driver. He served as a corps commander during the European fighting in World War II.

Kim Il Sung

Kim Il Sung was named premier of North Korea in 1948 and later (in 1972 under a new constitution) as president of the nation. Known as "Great Leader" in North Korea, he isolated the country from the outside world during his long tenure in office and then passed the reins of government to his son, Kim Jong Il.

General Oliver P. Smith

Historians have described General Smith's march out from the Chosin reservoir with his lst Marine Division as one of the greatest feats in military history. Historian Samuel Eliot Morison has compared it to the feat of the ancient Greek warrior Xenophon who, during a war with the Persians, marched 10,000 men through enemy-held territory from Babylon to the Black Sea.

General Matthew Ridgway

General Ridgway commanded the 82nd Airborne Division and the 18th Airborne Corps in Europe during World War II. In 1952 he departed Korea to serve as supreme commander of the North Atlantic Treaty Organization forces (NATO); taking his place in Korea was General Mark Clark. Ridgway became U.S. Army chief of staff a year later. He retired in 1955.

General Peng De-huai

Before becoming commander of the CCF in Korea, Peng had fought the Japanese in China before and during World War II and then the Nationalist forces of Chiang Kai-shek. He was a close friend and associate of North Korean Premier Kim Il Sung.

Parallel, be used instead. Since Kaesong was held by neither side and was thus on neutral ground, the UN Command agreed to the proposal.

Delegates from the warring sides met there on July 8 and made arrangements for the first of the armistice talks, which was then held on July 10. North Korea's General Nam Il headed the Communist delegation, and Admiral Turner C. Joy, the UN Command's ranking naval officer, led the United Nations group. On July 26 the negotiators completed the agenda of business meant to lead to an armistice. Its major points included:

- The establishment of a line of demarcation and a demilitarized zone between the opposing armies.

- The exchange of prisoners of war.

- The supervision of the armistice once an agreement was signed.

Though it seemed a simple one, the agenda led to one problem after another—snags that would cause the armistice talks to drag on for two years.

SNAGS AND HEATED WORDS

An early problem was an argument over the conference site. Kaesong fell into Communist hands as the talks were beginning, causing Admiral Joy to demand that he be given detailed assurances that the conference site would always remain neutral. Insulted, the Communists said that the assurances were not needed. The argument raged until October, with the talks being canceled twice—first, when a company of armed Communists entered the town and, next, when the Communist delegates angrily claimed that UN warplanes had bombed the place (a charge later proved to be false). The matter was finally settled when both sides agreed to shift the meeting site to the nearby village of Panmunjom.

Another argument flared over the establishment of the line of demarcation and the demilitarized zone. The Communists wanted the 38th Parallel to serve as the line, while Joy's team insisted that it be based on the battlefield positions of the armies at the time the armistice was signed. This argument prompted the small-scale attacks that marked the latter half of 1951 and then 1952, as each side fought to gain territory that would prove advantageous when peace came. Finally, in November, in trade for certain UN concessions they wanted, the Communists agreed to a line to be based on battlefield positions. It was also agreed that the opposing armies would drop back to form a demilitarized zone 2.5 miles (4 kilometers) wide and 250 miles (402 kilometers) long between them.

For a time, the negotiations went well. But one day in 1952 the Communists abruptly changed their ways. They began to object to every point on which there had been prior agreement. The change puzzled the UN team until word of a development at home reached Korea. With his popularity at a low ebb due to the snail's pace of the talks, the public's disgust with the war, and charges of underhanded political dealings by certain officials in his administration, President Truman announced his withdrawal from the November election for the presidency. Obviously, the Communists were out to delay the negotiations in the hope that they could win some advantages from a new U.S. leader.

It was a futile hope. Dwight D. Eisenhower won the November election and entered the White House in January 1953. As he had promised during his campaign, he visited Korea (a three-day trip) but did not make any specific suggestions to help the search for an armistice.

THE PRISONER EXCHANGE

The agenda item that triggered the greatest trouble was the one involving the exchange of prisoners of war (POWs). Held by the UN Command were some 132,000 Chinese and North Korean prisoners. Of that number, 49,000 expressed the desire to remain in South Korea. The Communist negotiators wanted all POWs returned home, no matter what their feelings. But the UN team argued that those who shunned repatriation were asking for political asylum and could not be forced to return. The exchange had to be made on a voluntary basis.

The Communists continued to insist on a forced return until March 28, 1953, when they suddenly agreed to the voluntary plan, doing so for two reasons. First, both sides were sick of the conflict and wanted it done with. The Chinese were especially troubled; they realized they were being bled dry financially by the costs of the war. Second, the recent death of Soviet Premier Josef Stalin had taken the USSR's mind off the global spread of communism for the moment. The USSR was now beset with internal problems that made it eager to be rid of a foreign war.

The exchange got under way in April, when each side began returning sick and wounded prisoners, with the main exchange, called the "Big Switch," to come later. The beginning trade, nicknamed "Little Switch," returned 5,194 North Koreans, 1,034 Chinese, and 445 civilians to the Communists, with the United Nations Command receiving 471 ROKs, 149 Americans, 32 Britons, 15 Turks, and 17 men from other UN countries. The trade gave the world hope that the last barrier to an armistice had been surmounted and that peace was at hand. Then there was more trouble.

In June, ROK President Syngman Rhee disrupted the exchange. Without warning, he released 27,000 North Korean POWs and told the South Korean people to give them shelter. He angrily claimed that the United States had betrayed him throughout the peace talks by not pressing his demand that the Communists give him what he had always wanted—the reunification of Korea under his government. The sudden release of the NK prisoners was meant to stop the peace process and bring his demand to the forefront.

In an attempt to strengthen his hand, he pulled his troops out of the UN Command and had his supporters stage angry anti-American demonstrations in Seoul. He sent them storming through the capital with signs emblazoned with the words "Go Home, Damned Yankees."

As Rhee had hoped, his actions infuriated both sides and halted the peace talks. But his demand for a reunified Korea went ignored. The talks remained stalled until July, when President Eisenhower, disgusted with the Korean leader's disruptive tactics, sent a representative to him with some blunt talk. The representative told Rhee that reunification was out of the question at present, that America would not assist him in fighting to reunite the peninsula, and that he was helpless to take over the North on his own. However, if Rhee would cooperate in bringing the peace talks to a conclusion, the United States would help him rebuild his army to twenty divisions and provide him with long-term economic aid. The assistance would begin with a shipment of 10 million pounds (4.5 million kilograms) of food and an immediate payment of $200 million. Rhee nodded in reluctant agreement.

The negotiations resumed on July 10 amid hard fighting as the opposing armies sought to better their final battlefield positions. Seventeen days later, on July 27, 1953, the armistice agreement was signed by Lieutenant General William K. Harrison (who had replaced Admiral Joy as the delegation leader) for the United Nations Command and by General Nam Il for the North Korean government. Each signed three copies, Harrison in blue ink and Nam Il in red.

At last, the guns fell silent.

AFTERMATH—THE "BIG SWITCH"

On August 5, just two weeks after silence returned, the main exchange of prisoners—the "Big Switch"—began. It continued until September 6. Released by the "Big Switch" and the earlier "Little Switch" were 118,917 men.

Freed by the UN Command were 70,183 North Koreans and 5,640 Chinese. More than 22,000 enemy soldiers refused to return home—14,704 Chinese and 7,900 North Koreans, all preferring to stay out of Communist hands. In total, 98,422 enemy troops were released.

The UN Command received 12,773 POWs: 7,862 ROKs, 3,597 Americans, 945 Britons, 227 Turks, and 140 men from the other UN nations. Of their number, 335 South Koreans refused to be repatriated, as did 23 Americans and 1 Briton. Two of the Americans later decided to return home.

THE DEAD AND WOUNDED

When the U.S prisoners were freed and went home, they left behind a peninsula country that lay in ruins, with its cities, towns, and villages devastated by the war. Killed and injured in the three years of fighting were more than 2 million North and South Koreans.

Closely matching that toll were the military losses recorded by both sides. A count made at the time held that the North Koreans suffered 625,264 casualties while the Chinese sustained 909,607, for a total of 1,534,871. The NK

A scene in Times Square, New York, when the truce is announced.

casualties amounted to 214,899 killed, 308,685 wounded, and 101,680 missing. The Chinese total came to 401,401 killed, 486,995 wounded, and 21,211 missing.

On the UN side, the South Koreans sustained 272,975 casualties: 46,812 killed, 159,727 wounded, and 66,436 missing. Of the nations that came to South Korea's aid, America contributed the most personnel and suffered the greatest losses, a total of 139,272: 24,965 dead, 101,368 wounded, and 12,939 missing. The fifteen UN nations that fought alongside the United States suffered 14,103 casualties: 2,597 killed, 9,581 wounded, and 1,925 missing.

In all, the casualties recorded by both sides came to a staggering 1,961,221. With the deaths and wounds suffered by the Korean population, the war killed and maimed more than 4 million people.

As is true of any war, the most tragic consequence of the Korean War was the loss of life. But the economic cost was also high. By itself, the United States spent more than $15 billion on the fighting, making Korea the third most expensive conflict in American history, surpassed only by World War II and the Vietnam conflict.

THE WAR THAT NOBODY WON

The Korean struggle has long been known as "the war that nobody won"—a name that is partially deserved because no outright victor ever emerged from Korea. But certain laurels were won by America and the United Nations. For one, the United States, in coming boldly to South Korea's defense, proved itself an international leader willing to act decisively against Communist aggression. Likewise, the United Nations, in its support of South Korea, enhanced its image on the world scene. At the time, the organization was being widely criticized for its inability to curb the spread of communism and was in danger of being disbanded. Its action on South Korea's behalf restored the UN's reputation and enabled it to continue its work in the coming decades.

But all sides suffered long-term problems because of the war. It intensified the hatred felt by the North and South Koreans for each other. It put a strain on U.S. relations with China that was to last until the 1990s and the opening of trade between the two countries. It caused a significant change in the type of aid that the United States would give to nations being threatened by aggression. Prior to Korea, that aid had been economic. But, with Korea, military aid was added to the assistance and led to the use of American troops in the horror that was the Vietnam conflict.

Over the decades since 1953, South Korea flowered while North Korea met with disaster. South Korea rebuilt itself into a prosperous democratic state with a strong international trade. But North Korea, under the rule of Kim Il Sung and then his son, became an isolated nation with little foreign trade and no use for the world's democratic states. As a result, it has long suffered a weak economy. In the 1990s it endured a severe drought that brought widespread starvation and death. Since 1995, North Korea has accepted $60.4 million in food from its great enemy, the United States.

The late 1990s also brought major economic problems for South Korea. The nation accepted a massive loan from the International Money Fund to rebuild its economy.

THE WAR THAT HAS NEVER ENDED

Quite accurately, the Korean conflict is also remembered as "the war that has never ended." The armistice of 1953 was to be the first step along the way to a peace agreement that would formally end the struggle. But no such pact has ever been arranged. To this day, the border between North and South Korea remains one of the most heavily militarized in the world, with about 1 million North Koreans staring across it at some 850,000 ROK and 37,000 American troops.

But the war may yet be formally ended one day. In August 1997, North Korean leaders, desperately worried about the drought plaguing their country, met with representatives from South Korea, the United States, and China to discuss the setting of an agenda for talks leading to a formal peace pact. The pact would open world trade to North Korea, help offset the terrible consequences of the drought, and perhaps bring a new prosperity to the country.

But, with hatreds still aflame after more than forty years, will it be possible ever to arrange a final peace pact? And, if so, when?

These are questions that no one can answer. But perhaps one future day will bring the answers.

BIBLIOGRAPHY

Alexander, Bevin. *Korea: The First War We Lost*. New York: Hippocrene Books, 1986.

Blair, Clay. *The Forgotten War: America in Korea 1950–1953*. New York: Times Books, 1987.

Brady, James. *The Coldest War: A Memoir of Korea*. New York: Orion Books, 1990.

Carnes, Mark C., and John A. Garraty, with Patrick Williams. *Mapping America's Past: A Historical Atlas*. New York: Henry Holt, 1996.

Collins, J. Lawton. *War in Peacetime: The History and Lessons of Korea*. Boston: Houghton Mifflin, 1969.

Garraty, John A., and Peter Gay, Editors. *The Columbia History of the World*. New York: Harper & Row, 1972.

Gosfield, Frank, and Bernhardt J. Hurwood. *Korea: Land of the 38th Parallel*. New York: Parent's Magazine Press, 1969.

Goulden, Joseph C. *Korea: The Untold Story of the War*. New York: Times Books, 1982.

Greenville, J. A. S. *The History of the World in the Twentieth Century*. Cambridge, Massachusetts: Belknap Press of Harvard University Press, 1994.

Halberstram, David. *The Fifties*. New York: Villard Books, 1993.

Hastings, Max. *The Korean War*. New York: Simon & Schuster, 1997.

Hoyt, Edwin P. *The Day the Chinese Attacked: Korea 1950*. New York: McGraw-Hill, 1990.

Leckie, Robert. *The Wars of America, Volume 2: From 1900 to 1992* (Updated Edition). New York: HarperCollins, 1992.

Link, Arthur S. *American Epoch: A History of the United States Since the 1890s*. New York: Knopf, 1959.

Manchester, William. *American Caesar: Douglas MacArthur 1880–1964*. Boston: Little, Brown, 1978.

McCullough, David. *Truman*. New York: Simon & Schuster, 1992.

Morison, Samuel Eliot. *The Oxford History of the American People, Volume 3: 1869–1963*. New York: New American Library, 1972.

Nevins, Allan, and Henry Steele Commager. *A Short History of the United States*, Fifth Edition, revised. New York: Modern Library, 1969.

Sheldon, Walt. *Hell or High Water: MacArthur's Landing at Inchon*. New York: Macmillan, 1968.

Spanier, John W. *The Truman-MacArthur Controversy and the Korean War*. New York: Norton, 1965.

Toland, John. *In Mortal Combat: Korea 1950–1953*. New York: Morrow, 1991.

INDEX

Page numbers in *italics* refer to illustrations.